THE
FINANCIAL
MATRIX

New York Times Bestselling Author

Orrin Woodward

Obstaclés Press and the Obstaclés logo are trademarks of LIFE Leadership.

Published by:

Obstaclés Press
200 Commonwealth Court
Cary, NC 27511

orrinwoodward.com

ISBN: 978-0-9961843-3-5

First Edition, April 2015
10 9 8 7 6 5 4 3 2 1

Scripture quotations marked "KJV" are taken from The Holy Bible, Cambridge, 1769.

Scripture quotations marked "NIV" are taken from The Holy Bible, New International Version®, NIV®, Copyright © 1973, 1978, 1984, 2011 by Biblica, Inc.® Used by permission of Biblica, Inc.® All rights reserved worldwide.

Cover and text design by Norm Williams, nwa-inc.com

Printed in the United States of America

Wars in old times were made to get slaves. The modern implement of imposing slavery is debt.

—Ezra Pound

Contents

CHAPTER 1
Our Story   9
Until Debt Do Us Part

CHAPTER 2
The Financial Matrix   19
Early Financial Matrices
The Creation of Money
Fractional-Reserve Banking (FRB) Equals Fool's Gold
The Truth Shall Set You Free

CHAPTER 3
Warren Buffett's Billionaire Lessons   33
Warren Buffett's Two Keys to Financial Success
Leadership Hard Skills versus Soft Skills
Expenses versus Investments

CHAPTER 4
Sam Walton: Building Business Assets   43
Sam Walton: Building Leaders and
    Turnkey Business Systems
Developing a Leadership Culture
Turnkey Business Operations

CHAPTER 5
Robert Kiyosaki and The Billionaire's   53
Three Keys to Wealth
The Mentors and the Plan

CHAPTER 6
Long-Term Vision   59
    The Ant and the Elephant
    Action: Where the Rubber Meets the Road
    Quitters, Campers, and Climbers
    Tim and Amy Marks: Long-Term Vision

CHAPTER 7
Delayed Gratification   73
    Employee Quadrant: "Per Hour" Pros and Cons
    Self-Employed Quadrant: "Per Task" Pros and Cons
    Business Owner Quadrant: "Per Relationship" Pros
        and Cons
    Investor Quadrant: "Per ROI" Pros and Cons
    Dan and Lisa Hawkins' Story

CHAPTER 8
Utilize the Power of Compounding   91
    Home-Based Business (HBB)
    The Internet
    Distribution
    Franchising Model
    The 3 Cs for Successful Internet Companies
    Content
    Commerce
    Community
    Claude and Lana Hamilton's Story
    Summary

Frequently Asked Questions   103

Morpheus: *Do you believe in fate, Neo?*

Neo: *No.*

Morpheus: *Why?*

Neo: *Because I don't like the idea that I'm not in control of my own life.*

Morpheus: *I know...exactly what you mean. Let me tell you why you're here. You're here because you know something. What you know you can't explain. But you feel it. You've felt it your entire life. That there's something wrong with the world. You don't know what it is, but it's there...like a splinter in your mind, driving you mad. It is this feeling that has brought you to me. Do you know what I'm talking about?*

Neo: *The [Financial] Matrix?*

Morpheus: *Do you want to know…what it is…? (Neo nods yes.) The Matrix is everywhere. It's all around us, even in this very room. You can see it when you look out your window or when you turn on your television. You can feel it when you go to work, when you go to church, when you pay your taxes. The [Financial] Matrix is the world that has been pulled over your eyes, to blind you from the truth.*

Neo: *What truth?*

Morpheus: *That you are a slave, Neo. Like everyone else, you were born into bondage, born into a prison that you cannot smell or taste or touch. A prison… for your mind….Unfortunately, no one can be…told what the [Financial] Matrix is….You have to see it for yourself.*

—PARAPHRASED FROM *THE MATRIX*, 1999 MOVIE SCRIPT[1]

CHAPTER 1

OUR STORY

It happened over twenty-two years ago, but it seems like yesterday. I had just walked in the door from a long day of work when Laurie excitedly announced that we were pregnant. Talk about an emotional jolt! On one hand, I was pumped, happy to be starting our family. On the other hand, however, I was worried. My brain had quickly calculated the economic implications of Laurie's message, and it didn't look good. Nonetheless, I didn't want to ruin the festive moment, so I wrapped my arms around Laurie and hid my growing angst as joy and fear battled for emotional supremacy.

One of the key selling points in convincing Laurie to marry me had been my expected income as a successful engineer. Accordingly, I promised Laurie she could be a stay-at-home mom once we started our family. Of course, this promise (and many others) was made before we got married and accumulated thirty-two thousand dollars of consumer debt outside of our mortgage. In truth, I couldn't figure out how we were going to make it without her income, especially since I knew children would only add to our already inflated expenses. There was simply no way we could lose Laurie's income, add expenses for children, and still pay our bills.

Sadly, like the proverbial ostrich with its head in the sand, I refused to face reality. Instead, I somehow believed that if I ignored the issue long enough, Laurie would just continue working until I cleaned up our financial mess. In fact, in my more optimistic moments, I even thought Laurie wanted to keep working (she was a professional accountant, after all) and that she wouldn't hold me accountable for the promises made during the courting process. My optimism, however, was not founded upon facts. After several weeks of strategic silence, Laurie finally lost her patience and dropped the bomb. One evening, despite knowing I had to go to class that night, Laurie flat out asked me when she should notify her employer about leaving her job. This was it. The moment I had hoped to avoid was now upon me, and I could feel my heart rate increasing in anticipation.

Needless to say, I was not a happy camper. Nonetheless, I breathed deeply and moved right into my rehearsed line about how bad our finances were and how it wasn't the right time for her to leave her job. Laurie, evidently having practiced her lines as well, simply said, "Orrin, you promised me." I attempted to deflect this inarguable truth by agreeing in principle but repeating that the timing wasn't right. Laurie, however, was not messing around. Again, she said, "Orrin, you promised me." Facts are pesky things, and no matter how badly I wanted to deny Laurie's statement, she was stating a fact. Disoriented, I couldn't even look her in the eyes this time as I mumbled something about bills and timing. Laurie wasn't buying what I was selling. Once more, she simply looked me in the eyes and said, "You promised me." That ended the argument—game, set, match! How could I argue with the truth? I meekly agreed to honor my promise even though I had no idea how to do so.

Strangely, I felt relieved after our discussion. Sure, the financial issue wasn't resolved, but the moral one was. I had made a promise, and I intended to keep it. I hustled to my car and headed down to the University of Michigan for my night class. The next hour and a half was a series of lectures directed to my steering wheel. I asked myself what turn I had missed to land in this financial ditch. No matter how many accolades I had received (honor society in college, attending the #2 ranked MBA program, four US patents, and a National Technical Benchmarking award), I still had to admit that they weren't paying the bills. It was time to confront brutal reality. Even though, like most other men of my generation, I had diversified my income by sending my wife to work, we still lived paycheck to paycheck. I thought to myself, if two upwardly mobile professionals couldn't make ends meet, how was everyone else doing it? In short, my rose-colored financial glasses were permanently cracked. I later learned that most others weren't making it either. That night however, I focused on fulfilling the promise I had made to Laurie, even if I needed to get another job. That night changed my life. I vowed to no longer accept conventional wisdom without dealing with the consequences of following the advice myself. Ironically, as an engineer, I taught the principle "In God we trust; all others must have data." Yet until that night, I had never applied this principle to my finances.

Until Debt Do Us Part

Later, after studying the dismal financial status of people across the civilized world, I realized Laurie and I were not alone. Practically everyone with student loans, car loans, credit cards, and home mortgages was drowning in a sea of debt. Personal solvency had become an increasingly difficult proposition in these financially turbulent times. Indeed, the latest American debt numbers are shocking.* According to GoBankingRates, an organization which tracks interest and banking rates, the average American in 2014 was more than $225,000 in debt, and almost half US households had less than $500 in savings.

Here is a summary of the American statistics organized by category of debt:

- Average credit card debt among indebted households: $15,263
- Average credit card interest rate: 14.95% APR
- Average mortgage debt: $147,591
- Average outstanding student loan balance: $31,646
- Average auto loan debt: $30,738
- Percentage of Americans with at least $500 in a savings account: 59%˙

When the average debt numbers are multiplied by the average interest rates, one arrives at the astounding figure of $1,500 per month; this is the amount of money that the average family must pay just to service debt. However, servicing debt doesn't decrease debt; it merely pays the *interest* on the debt so the household can use what it cannot afford to own. In order to pay $1,500 per month, a person must make $2,000 per month, and this only assumes a 25% tax rate. In other words, the average family loses the first $24,000 they earn per year just to service debt from things they do not own. Unbelievable and unsustainable!

---

* The data from around the civilized world are equally alarming.

Unfortunately, the bad news gets even worse. According to the Internal Revenue Service's (IRS) data, the real (inflation adjusted) median household income for 2013 was $51,939. This may sound impressive until one remembers that the average family uses the first $24,000 (almost half of the average income) to service its debts. This leaves around $28,000 per household to live on. Adding insult to injury, household income has been trending downward (a drop of nearly 8%) since its 1999 peak of $56,895. In other words, average Americans have worked for less income than when they started for sixteen consecutive years.

That's not all. While household incomes are trending downward, inflation is skyrocketing prices upward. Anyone remember five-and-dime stores? Today, they are dollar stores that somehow get away with selling items for ten dollars or more. Lower pay, increased prices, and increased debts are a knockout combination against workers. Imagine people working for sixteen consecutive years for less money as prices increase yearly and then having to make up the income/price gap by taking on additional debt. Sadly, the worst part about this scenario is that it isn't imagination but today's reality.

Above all, however, one must remember that the average household income combines the incomes from *everyone* in the household who is making money. Consequently, the average *person's* income is even less impressive than the average *household's*. In fact, according to the 2014 IRS data, the average American made $33,048. Here are the top American percentages:

- Top 1% - $380,354
- Top 5% - $159,619
- Top 10% - $113,799

- Top 25% - $67,280
- Top 50% - $33,048

When the average income figures are placed side-by-side with the average debt figures, the modern debt disaster is revealed. Indeed, it is practically impossible for families to make ends meet without both husband and wife working. For instance, to be in the top 25% of income earners in the USA, according to the 2014 IRS statistics, one only has to make $67,280! This is barely enough income to service the average debt (and typically, higher incomes take on more debt for bigger houses and better cars). Even the top 10% of Americans at $113,799 are still on the edge of financial solvency since a person who makes more also qualifies for more loans. And, without financial discipline, more income leads to more loans which can produce even bigger debt dangers.

However, this debt spiral is not just a financial issue; it's also causing undue levels of stress and anxiety. According to a 2014 study of over 3,000 American adults by the American Psychological Association (APA), 72% of Americans said they felt stressed about money at some point during the previous month, and 26% said they felt stressed about their finances most or all of the time. Furthermore, 54% admitted they had "just enough" or "not enough" money to meet their monthly needs. High debts and low income are acting as a vice squeezing the lifeblood from the people. Is anyone else concerned when over half of the respondents admit to running out of money before they run out of month? Regretfully, the *economics* of debt ensure the mess will only get worse unless the people wake up—because the people's debt is the lender's profit. And since the American Psychology Association (APA) survey confirmed the pain debt is causing Americans, it's as if the old saying "no pain, no gain" has been changed by the banks to read "your pain is our gain." Or, more pointedly, "Your pain is our profit." Incredibly, the APA survey can be summarized: the banks produce profits by delivering pain.

*Debt is like any other trap, easy enough to get into,
but hard enough to get out of.*

—HENRY WHEELER SHAW

CHAPTER 2

THE FINANCIAL MATRIX

Society's debt, however, isn't just about profits and pain. It's also about control. When a person views the financial system through the lens of profits and control for the aristocratic elites and subsequent stress and oppression for the masses, he is beginning to comprehend the Financial Matrix. Remarkably, the principles of the Financial Matrix are not new, for Proverbs 22:7 (NIV) reads, "The rich rule over the poor, and the borrower is slave to the lender." When a person is in debt, he or she is in bondage. Lenders, disgracefully, change the Biblical Golden Rule "Do unto others as you would have them do unto you" into a new Golden Rule: "He who has the gold makes the rules." Curiously, however, the Financial Matrix doesn't force people into debt enslavement; instead, it *tempts* them into it. Indeed, modern marketing campaigns are so effective that many enslave themselves by purchasing things they cannot afford. While this may sound harsh, the humorous (much truth is told in jest) jingle "I owe; I owe; it's off to work I go" conveys a similar message. No one is forced into buying what he or she cannot afford; instead, people fall for the alluring advertisements and seductive slogans. These high-priced marketing campaigns are specifically designed to make the unreasonable appear reasonable, namely, submit to slavery so you can use what you cannot afford to own.

The Financial Matrix was formed when Big Governments, Big Banks, and Big Corporations killed the gold standard (asset money) and rebooted the monetary system based on debt money. As people sell themselves into debt, the Financial Matrix increases its profits and control. Like I said earlier, the masses' pain (debt and stress) is the elites' gain (profits and control).

Once we understood the scope of the Financial Matrix, Laurie and I adjusted our financial goals. And no longer did we simply want to escape the Matrix personally; we wanted to help others do the same. For just as Edmund Burke is credited with writing, "All that is necessary for the triumph, of evil is that good men do nothing," we knew that doing nothing was not an option. Please don't misunderstand me; it doesn't take a conspiracy for companies to maximize profits, but it does take an education for consumers to minimize pain. Instead of rallying the masses to protest against the Financial Matrix, Laurie and I focused on educating the masses and helping those who would help themselves.

> **It doesn't take a conspiracy for companies to maximize profits, but it does take an education for consumers to minimize pain.**

For over twenty years, I have researched the political, economic, and social histories of Western Civilization, and I have arrived at some startling conclusions. Perhaps the biggest is that the aristocratic elites of every generation have sought a control matrix of some type to exploit the production of the masses. This may appear radical at first, but please hear me out. The famous French political philosopher Bertrand de Jouvenel said something similar when he noted (with brackets added by me):

> Whoever does not wish to render history incomprehensible by departmentalizing it—political, economic, social—would perhaps take the view that it is in essence a battle of dominant wills [elites], fighting in every way they can for the material which is common to everything they construct: the human labor force [masses].

In other words, the aristocratic elites (dominant wills) seek methods to control the masses' production (human labor). Viewing history through this lens, I then reviewed my notes from the economic field and recalled the three factors needed for all production: labor, land, and capital. Indeed, one of the classical economists, John Stuart Mill, wrote, "The Law of the Increase of Production depends on those of Three Elements—**Labor**, **Capital**, and **Land**." When I married these two concepts together, I realized I had discovered the aristocracy's playbook for the matrices of control throughout history. In order for the elites to control the masses' production, they must do so by controlling one (or more) of the three factors of production. Not surprisingly, history reveals the aristocracy used each of the three factors of production in building the three main control matrices used throughout history.

Early Financial Matrices

Needless to say, the Financial Matrix was not the aristocracy's first matrix of control. Rather, it's the third one (based upon the third factor of production) created after the first two matrices (based upon the first two factors of production) collapsed. Interestingly, most people are likely familiar with the other two matrices of control: the Physical Matrix (human slavery) and the Land Matrix (feudal serfdom). Ironically, although the Greeks and Romans, Western Civilization's founders, wrote about liberty and justice extensively, they also hypocritically exercised the Physical Matrix to enslave defeated foes. The slaves were forced to work, while the conquerors, who disdained physical work, enjoyed the liberty to speak, write, and lead. The Physical Matrix was a system of control in which the aristocracy (the strong) forced the masses (the weak) to toil away in slavery and obscurity. The Physical Matrix was the preferred method of control throughout antiquity until something changed in the late Roman Empire.

That change was the influence of Christianity upon the social norms of Roman society. Whereas slavery was previously acceptable, Christian doctrine taught that all men were created equal before an almighty God. Since all fellow believers were brothers and sisters in Christ, it became increasingly difficult to rationalize how a Christian could enslave a fellow brother or sister. (Unfortunately, the later discovery of America restored European rationalizations which led to the Physical Matrix enslavement of people from Africa.) Thus, without the moral support in European society, the Physical Matrix collapsed under its own weight during the Middle Ages. Not surprisingly, however, the aristocrats sought an alternative matrix of control to replace it. Since labor could no longer be controlled directly, perhaps the aristocracy could instead do indirectly what it could no longer do directly. Predictably, almost as if the aristocracy understood the three factors of production and crossed off the first one (labor) only to move on to the next one (land), the aristocracy built the Land Matrix by owning and controlling all the land during Europe's Middle Ages. The Land Matrix (feudal serfdom) was a system of control which empowered the aristocrats (kings, princes, and lords) with land, while the serfs were forced to serve a lord in order to survive.

Feudalism (the Land Matrix) was, in essence, a system which allowed the aristocrats to promise the serfs protection in exchange for the serfs working the aristocrats' lands. The new matrix provided the serf the land he needed to live for a land tax amounting to around 50% of his agricultural production. Furthermore, the serfs agreed to work the lord's fields several days a week, since the aristocrats rarely, if ever, worked their own fields. The serfs, having nowhere else to go and not having the strength to resist such tyranny, simply submitted to the Land Matrix. Although the serfs were technically no longer slaves, they weren't exactly free either; high taxes and forced immobility permitted the aristocrats to indirectly control the serfs' labor by directly controlling all the land. Generations of serfs would live and die on the same piece of land performing basically the same work as their forefathers. Feudalism in Europe ended the Physical Matrix slavery (control of the first factor of production—labor) only to birth the Land Matrix serfdom (control of the second factor of production—land).

Finally, however, during the late Middle Ages, the reintroduction of gold and silver destroyed the economics of feudalism, as the serfs no longer needed to live on the lord's land. The serfs migrated to the growing cities, where they became bakers, butchers, and candlestick makers. In the city air, the serf could breathe free. The peasants, instead of being stuck to the land, sold their services for gold and silver (asset money) and then traded the asset money to purchase other items necessary for survival. Asset money and free cities allowed the serfs to live without the lord's land, and, not shockingly, the Land Matrix collapsed. The serfs could no longer be controlled by the aristocrats, and now, the Physical and Land Matrices were, for all practical purposes, extinct.

However, there was still one more factor of production (capital) the aristocrats could seek to control in order to build another matrix. The battle between society's gold standard asset money and the aristocrat's fiat standard debt money began in earnest. Interestingly, money was created by society's members as a measurement of exchange of value. The following several paragraphs are an attempt to simplify a complicated subject. Thankfully, it's not crucial to understand all of this when reading it for the first time, but I want to include it so that people have access to the truth of our current financial system.

The Creation of Money

Money was created by society to measure what one item was worth in relation to others. Gold and silver were the preferred forms of money because they were scarce, easily divisible, mobile, and universally recognized. And since gold is a fixed quantity (it cannot be created out of thin air) and is difficult to mine, inflation (any increase in the total supply of gold) was low and predictable. Indeed, the rebirth of asset money fueled the growth of capitalism by increasing the division of labor and of trade between peoples. Remarkably, for nearly four hundred years, asset money led to the creation of more wealth for more people than at any time in recorded history.

Of course, the aristocrats attempted various methods to manipulate the money supply (debasement and fractional-reserve banking), but the gold standard tied their hands.

Indeed, any time the people suspected the aristocrats of foul play, they could demand all payments in gold, forcing the aristocrats to pay in asset money rather than in the manipulated debt money. The gold standard acted as an automatic regulator to protect the masses against the manipulations of the elites because it forced the elites to redeem their paper debt money into gold asset money whenever the paper holder demanded it. This on-demand gold standard redemption policy tempered the aristocrats' inflation manipulation ability because the elites feared the masses would cause a run on their banks if they suspected fraudulent overprinting of paper compared to gold reserves. The gold standard, in sum, was the only thing standing in the way of the elites' matrix of control over the third factor of production—capital.

Unfortunately, with the start of World War I, the elites finally smashed through the gold standard and achieved their four-hundred-year objective: the birth of the Financial Matrix through control of the third factor of production—capital. The four hundred years of expanding liberty now began its long contraction in the vice grip of fiat debt money and fractional-reserve banking. True, the wealth created over those four hundred years was not lost overnight, but slowly, painfully, and inexorably, debt money would replace assets, and control would replace liberty. The aristocrats' Financial Matrix created a system of indirect control of the masses' labor through the direct control of the medium of exchange (money) needed by all using the capitalistic system. One can easily see the damage caused by the Financial Matrix by studying

> **Slowly, painfully, and inexorably, debt money would replace assets, and control would replace liberty.**

the lost value of the US dollar since the 1913 creation of the Federal Reserve banking system in the United States. The value of one US dollar in 1913 is now worth less than four cents today. Put differently, it now takes twenty-five dollars to purchase what one dollar could purchase in 1913. Dismally, however, inflation is just one of many injustices caused by the Financial Matrix.

Fractional-Reserve Banking (FRB) Equals Fool's Gold

When inflation is combined with increased personal and national debts (which increase taxes), it's easy to understand why the masses across the civilized world struggle to make ends meet. Indeed, the government-sponsored fractional-reserve banking (FRB) system allows banks, in partnership with the central banks, to create the majority of society's money (debt money) out of thin air. Remarkably, the FRB system permits the banks to create fiat debt money but forces borrowers to pay it back with real assets earned through real production.

> The FRB system permits the banks to create fiat debt money but forces borrowers to pay it back with real assets earned through real production.

It's as if the banks have been given a license to produce fool's gold and pass it off as real gold. Accordingly, the banks manufacture the artificial fool's gold (fake FRB digitized debt) to loan to people who must pay back the loan and interest with real gold (actual production). In sum, FRB permits banks to create fools gold to control the fools.

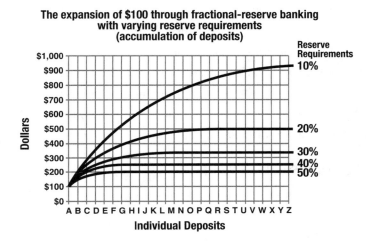

The expansion of $100 through fractional-reserve banking with varying reserve requirements (accumulation of deposits)

The Financial Matrix is the best form of control ever designed by the elites because it is difficult to detect. Whereas it was easy to see the coercion involved in slavery or serfdom (Physical Matrix and Land Matrix, respectively), few people understand that debt money is coercion created out of thin air. Debtors are forced to pay back fiat loans through performing real work. If they don't, they are invariably coerced through threats of litigation, bankruptcy, or shame. The FRB system is the key to the Financial Matrix and is why the latest matrix is the most effective and efficient one ever.

Above all else, remember that the Financial Matrix system of control is dependent upon the creation of debt money. As a result, the Financial Matrix promotes home ownership and home mortgages because that produces most of the system's debt money (approximately two-thirds of all US debt money is from home mortgages). Disastrously, the Financial Matrix has gutted home-equity percentages (amount of value remaining after subtracting all mortgage amounts owed), decreasing them from over 80% in the 1950s to just over 30% today. The Financial Matrix, essentially, has siphoned nearly 50% of the value of the USA's $25 trillion housing market in just the last sixty years! That equates to merely $12.5 trillion dollars (almost as much as the total US national debt) of assets lost by US citizens with little to show for it. And this story is much the same in other countries.

The Truth Shall Set You Free

Okay, I promise that was the most complicated part of the book! It explains why the Financial Matrix is so successful and why so few people understand it, let alone know how to resist it. In fact, this is why I started the book with a scene from the movie *The Matrix*. If you haven't watched it, I encourage you to do so. Perhaps no movie has ever before captured so much truth in the form of fiction. Neo is searching for answers to understand why he feels enslaved even though he is allegedly free. He spends his days working a job and his nights searching for answers to the paradox. Similarly, for the last twenty years, I have been building leadership companies as my business and searching for life's answers as my purpose. To me, the discovery of the Financial Matrix system of control is eerily similar to Neo's discovery of the Matrix. In a particularly telling scene, Morpheus explains to Neo why the world is not as it seems, that the Matrix exists to control the masses' energy (it's a sci-fi thriller, after all) whether they are working, playing, or sleeping. The Matrix is, as Morpheus explains to Neo, "The world that has been pulled over your eyes, to blind you from the truth."[2]

Of course, Neo asks what truth Morpheus is referring to and learns:

That you are a slave, Neo. Like everyone else, you
were born into bondage, born into a prison that you
cannot smell or taste or touch. A prison...for your
mind....Unfortunately, no one can be...told what the
(Financial) Matrix is....You have to see it for yourself.[3]

Morpheus places two pills before Neo and gives him a
choice. If he takes the blue pill, Neo will live an illusion and
never escape the Matrix. If he takes the red pill, he will learn
the truth about the Matrix and how to set himself free.

If you, like Neo, have been searching for answers, the good
news is that the search is over. Just as Morpheus offered Neo
the chance to learn the truth, so too do I offer you the truth.
The rest of the book explains the Financial Matrix and how
you can avoid it. If you read the book, you will discover how
deep the rabbit hole goes and how to escape it. If you don't read
the book, you can believe whatever you want to believe locked
inside the Financial Matrix. Not to sound overly dramatic, but
I truly believe your next move will have long-term financial
consequences.

For those moving ahead, it's time to share the billionaire
secrets that provided me the roadmap out of the Financial
Matrix.

The chains of habit are too light to be felt until they are too heavy to be broken.

—WARREN BUFFETT

CHAPTER 3

WARREN BUFFETT'S BILLIONAIRE LESSONS

To achieve financial mastery in life, one of the key decisions people must make is who they are going to listen to. There are two ways to ensure failure: (1) listen to everyone and (2) listen to no one. Personally, I was stuck in the Financial Matrix because everyone I was listening to was also trapped in the Matrix. Doesn't it make sense that people cannot mentor others beyond their personal financial results? Indeed, if people knew how to do better, wouldn't they have helped themselves first? For instance, even though I knew my parents loved me, I also finally realized they were only capable of teaching me to attain the same level of financial results they had achieved. Accordingly, I made a decision to love my parents but to stop taking financial advice from them and instead seek mentors who had freed themselves from the Financial Matrix.

Another key was realizing I had to stop taking my own advice. I had heard one of my early mentors say, "If you are not happy with the results you are producing, perhaps it's time to stop taking your own advice." Ouch! That one hurt, but Laurie and I learned our lesson. We started with the end in mind by determining the financial life we wanted and found people who already lived that way. We sought financial wisdom through attending seminars with successful people and when we couldn't be with them in person, we fed our minds a steady supply of books and audios from the people who had produced or were producing financial results. I believed that if one person could free him- or herself from the Financial Matrix, then Laurie and I could as well by applying the same principles and practices. Warren Buffett's advice that I mentioned earlier was a vital piece of the puzzle to help us change how we thought about money, time, and success.

Warren Buffett's Two Keys to Financial Success

Warren Buffett, in my opinion, is the greatest investment manager of all time. Although he didn't start with much, Buffett implemented disciplined spending habits (minimized expenses) and careful investment strategies (maximized investments) to compound his assets until he became one of the wealthiest people in the world. When Buffett discussed principles on expenses and investments, I was listening. For example, in a CNBC interview in front of an audience of college students, Warren Buffett gave the following advice:

> *CNBC:* "What is the one thing that young people should be doing about money?"
> *Buffett:* "I tell them two things, generally. One is to **stay away from credit cards.**...The second thing I tell them is to **invest in themselves.**" (Emphasis added.)

Buffett's short answer contained a ton of wisdom. I separated his advice into two main categories: First, live debt-free (play defense), and second, invest in yourself (play offense). Buffett helped me realize that financial success was not just living like a miser but, rather, minimizing expenses and maximizing investments. In another talk to college students, Buffett emphasized the importance of self-investment. He asked them if they would take $50,000 cash for 10% of their future income. When nearly half the students raised their hands to accept the offer, Buffett pointed out that they must believe they are worth at least $500,000 since 10% of $500,000 is $50,000. He then drove home the message by asking the students how many other $500,000 assets they currently had. Not shockingly, every hand went down. Buffett then concluded by stressing that your number one asset is yourself, so don't be cheap in investing in you. For some reason, I had a hard time with this one before Buffett's reasoning changed me. Sure, if my employer paid for school, I would go, but I didn't understand that I could not rise above my own leadership limitations. If I wanted to grow, then my leadership would have to grow. Buffett made me a believer in financial defense and offense, and it was a game changer for our family.

In yet another interview, Buffett talked about his two college diplomas and the Dale Carnegie certificate from attending a public speaking seminar. He told the interviewer that he had no idea where his degrees were, but he proudly displayed his Dale Carnegie certificate behind his desk. Interestingly, Buffett emphasized the importance of reading when he held up stacks of reading materials and stated, "Read 500 pages like this every day. That's how knowledge builds up, like compound interest."

If the greatest investment manager in the world believes personal education compounds just like traditional investments, then from then on, I would also be compounding my knowledge. In fact, the LIFE Leadership company was formed to teach Buffett's (and other billionaires') principles to others. The Financial Fitness Program (FFP), one of our most successful products, teaches people how to eliminate debt, and the LIFE Leadership monthly subscription series help people affordably invest in self-education. Once people learn that they are their greatest asset, they should immerse themselves in financial principles and leadership development and start thinking like billionaires rather than broke people.

Leadership Hard Skills versus Soft Skills

While technical hard skills are typically learned during one's formal education and supplemented with on-the-job training, soft skills are rarely taught in school or at work. Therefore, a potential leader must take personal responsibility for learning and applying the relational soft skills in his daily interactions with others. However, to do this properly, one must first understand the difference between a hard skill and a soft skill. Perhaps the simplest method for differentiating between the two types of skills is to consider hard skills as science and soft skills as art. Whereas science focuses on objective numerical outcomes that can be measured, art focuses on subjective aesthetic outcomes that must be experienced. Hard skills (like typing speed, engineering training, IQ level, or computer programming skills) can be measured objectively, while soft skills (like teamwork, patience, people skills, public speaking, and persistence) can only be measured subjectively.

> **Whereas science focuses on objective numerical outcomes that can be measured, art focuses on subjective aesthetic outcomes that must be experienced.**

While most people would think hard skills are more important than soft skills, scientific research reveals just the opposite. For instance, Google, in a study codenamed "Project

Oxygen," data-mined every performance review, feedback survey, and nomination for top-manager awards within the company. The search engine giant identified the eight most important skills for effective leadership and discovered that technical expertise ranked dead last out of the eight. Historically, Google's management strategy had been simple: leave the programmers alone and let them reach out to their bosses, who were promoted based upon their mastery of technical skills. However, according to Laszlo Bock, Google's Vice President of "Human Operations," Project Oxygen changed their mindset. "In the Google context, we'd always believed that to be a manager, particularly on the engineering side, you needed to be as deep or deeper a technical expert than the people who work for you," Mr. Bock says. "It turns out that that's absolutely the least important thing. It's important, but pales in comparison. Much more important is just making that connection and being accessible."

Once a person has the basic hard skills, then soft skills become the key differentiator in career advancement and leadership success. Interestingly, Google's findings are not really new but merely confirm statistically what was previously known intuitively, namely, that everything rises and falls on leadership. After all, in 1936, Dale Carnegie wrote, "...15 percent of one's financial success is due to one's technical knowledge and about 85 percent is due to skill in human engineering—to personality and the ability to lead people." True leaders, in essence, combine the science-side hard skills and the art-side soft skills to build leadership cultures of trust and influence. And every time people invest in themselves, they are building their number one asset. Improved soft skills help people build their most important asset, which improves their earnings potential irrespective of whether they are an employee, self-employed, or a business owner. Buffett taught me the importance of spending less than I make (defense) and investing the difference in assets (offense), beginning with myself. Since everything rises and falls on leadership, Laurie and I knew we needed to grow our leadership abilities in order to grow our business. The only sustainable competitive advantage in today's competitive marketplace is the leadership team's ability to learn faster than the competition.

Expenses versus Investments

Perhaps more than anything else, Buffett taught me the difference between an expense and an investment. Financially speaking, this distinction is what separates the wealthy from the poor. An expense is money, spent with no expectations of a return, whereas an investment is money invested for an expected return. Money poured into proper investments produces additional money while money poured into expenses is simply wasted. Wealthy people maximize investments (in themselves and in business) while minimizing all expenses. In contrast, the poor minimize investments (in themselves and business) while maximizing expenses. In other words, being poor is not so much an income as it is a mindset (and the results of the habits that come from that mindset). One can be poor making $50,000, $100,000, or $200,000 per year. It's not how much a person makes but rather how much goes to investment versus expenses that determines whether one is poor. An investment is anything that will eventually have a

> An expense is money spent with no expectations of a return, whereas an investment is money invested for an expected return.

return, while an expense is money poured down the drain. The reason Buffett is the greatest investment manager of all time is because he has utilized a higher percentage of his money in investments to compound consistently over time than any other person.

Everyone is familiar with the story of David and Goliath. I like to draw on that story from time to time because it makes for such a universal visual. To succeed at the game of life, people must see life as a series of Goliaths placed in their path to test their faith. When one Goliath is defeated, the victory advances a person up the leadership mountain. The more people exercise their faith, even when they are afraid, they become a Goliath slayer (achiever) rather than a Goliath circler (procrastinator). Laurie and I were so off-track in our investments and expenses that we knew it was the first Goliath assigned to us to slay.

Looking back, it's no wonder Laurie and I struggled financially. In effect, we did the exact opposite of billionaires with respect to money, expenses, and investments. We maximized entertainment expenses using credit cards, car loans, and same-as-cash impulse buying, and we minimized investments by having no business, no personal development plan, and thus, no tax benefits from having our own business. Either we would change our mindset about money, or we would always lack the funds to invest in ourselves and in building a business. Fortunately, we followed through on our commitment to change. First, I tapped into my 401(k) retirement plan to borrow $5,000 from myself in order to start our first business (offense). Second, we cut every expense that wasn't absolutely necessary to live (canceled cable television, sold new cars to drive used, stopped eating out, etc.) and eliminated debt over the next several years.

We were done playing small! We had our long-term vision: get free from the Financial Matrix and enjoy a millionaire lifestyle without credit of any kind, including home mortgages. And we committed to one another to play defense like champions. In fact, Laurie read the section in Thomas Stanley's book *The Millionaire Next Door* (in which he identifies the wife's spending habits as one of the key factors in wealth accumulation) so many times she could practically repeat it from memory. Laurie, because she had long-term vision, successfully delayed her gratification, and today she is enjoying the benefits from our decade of discipline. Whether you choose to play solely defense (a twenty-to-thirty-year plan to get out of the Financial Matrix) or choose to play both defense and offense (generally a two-to-five-year plan out), the important thing is to start today. The sooner you start, the sooner you can change compound interest from working against you to working for you. The only thing you have to lose is your debt!

Now that we have discussed the importance of eliminating debt (defense) and investing in yourself (offense, part 1), it's time to learn about building a business asset (offense, part 2).

Two things about Sam Walton distinguish him from almost anyone else that I know. First, he gets up every day bound and determined to improve something. Second, he is less afraid of being wrong than anyone I've ever known. And once he sees he's wrong, he just shakes it off and heads in another direction.

—DAVID GLASS, FORMER CEO OF WAL-MART

CHAPTER 4

SAM WALTON: BUILDING BUSINESS ASSETS

Building a business asset is the fastest way to break free from the time-for-money trap. In this chapter, I am going to share what I learned from Sam Walton, the founder of Wal-Mart, about building a business asset. The two keys are:

- Developing people
- Developing turnkey systems

Indeed, when you combine Buffett's financial principles with Walton's business principles, you are developing a plan to break out of the Financial Matrix. When built properly, a business asset produces income through relationships and systems instead of the number of hours or tasks performed.

Unfortunately, few have learned these principles because they are not taught in any traditional educational program. As a matter of fact, only people who have built a business asset are qualified to teach others how to do the same. For this reason, it's time to learn how to build a business asset from one of the most successful business people of the twentieth century and the one I learned from, Sam Walton.

Sam Walton: Building Leaders and Turnkey Business Systems

Today, Wal-Mart is a huge conglomerate of stores across the world, but few remember Sam Walton's "David versus Goliath" historical origins. In 1952, four new entrants joined the discount store market and three of them were backed by billion-dollar entities: K-Mart supported by the Kresge fortune, Woolco supported by Woolworth money, and Target supported by Dayton-Hudson. The fourth new entrant, Wal-Mart, barely had enough money to launch its first store, and the founder himself raised 95% of the money personally. This appeared to be a rigged match, yet somehow Walton won anyway. How was that possible? How did Sam Walton, despite competing in a business model that required massive front-end funding with relative pennies to his competitors' dollars, defeat his billionaire foes so convincingly? Whether you admire the Wal-Mart of today is not important, but what is vitally important is to understand how Walton built his business asset in such a manner that it walked over much bigger competitors. As such, I have read practically everything I could get my hands on about Walton and Wal-Mart to determine what made his business asset so successful. Accordingly, I identified two things that he did better than anyone else, as stated above: build leaders and build turnkey business systems. In reality, every business asset must build people and systems, but Walton did both of them better than anyone else.

Developing a Leadership Culture

Sam Walton believed that a successful business asset must consistently find and build people. He invested significant amounts of time finding the right people, setting high standards for them, and serving them to help everyone win—owners, associates, and customers. Walton emphasized the importance of leadership when he said, "I needed somebody to run my new store, and I didn't have much money, so I did something I would do for the rest of my run in the retail business without any shame or embarrassment whatsoever: nose around other people's stores searching for good talent." Talent, however, without teamwork can lead to disaster, so Walton encouraged new leaders to: "Submerge your own ambitions and help whoever you can in the company. Work together as a team." To build a leadership culture of this caliber, the top leader must focus his or her efforts on serving others.

Once Walton had the right people on the bus and in the right seats, he stressed the importance of communication by saying, "Communicate, communicate, communicate....We do it in so many ways, from the Saturday morning meeting to the very simple phone call to our satellite system. The necessity for good communication in a big company like this is so vital it can't be overstated." Moreover, although he used technology to gather data and communicate his message, he never allowed "high-tech" to replace the people's need for "high-touch." Indeed, Walton emphasized, "A computer is not—and will never be—a substitute for getting out in your stores and learning what's going on. In other words, a computer can tell you down to the dime what you've sold. But it can never tell you how much you could have sold." This was the difference between the managers at his billion-dollar competitors and the leader Walton was. The manager attempts to have high-tech do what only high-touch can achieve, namely, inspire the human heart to achieve something bigger than itself.

Finally, Walton understood that in order to win consistently in business, the customer must be satisfied. He stated, "Everything we've done since we started Wal-Mart has been devoted to this idea that the customer is our boss....We have never doubted our philosophy that the customer comes ahead of everything else." With the customer satisfied, Walton was then in a position to satisfy his associates who worked with him by developing people and systems. He believed in win-win compensation arrangements to inspire his people to consistently raise the bar on themselves. He wrote, "The more you share profits with your associates—whether it's in salaries or incentives or bonuses or stock discounts—the more profit will accrue to the company. Why? Because the way management treats the associates is exactly how the associates will then treat the customers." Walton created a leadership culture by finding, building, and leading people who bought into his vision of serving his customers. He built a world-class leadership culture that continued to perform impressively after his death. However, what made Wal-Mart capable of defeating Goliath-sized competitors was his marrying of the best leadership culture to the best turnkey business operating system.

Turnkey Business Operations

Impressively, Walton implemented a turnkey business operation that produced superior results as much by predictable systems as with superior people. Indeed, study any billionaire business model, and you will find a turnkey business system

> **The more predictable the business system, the more predictable the business results.**

producing repeatable results for anyone who leverages the system. The more predictable the business system, the more predictable the business results. In essence, successful businesses eliminate chaos by creating predictable processes that lead to successful results. Author Michael Gerber explains:

> Once the franchisee learns the system, he is given the key to his own business. Thus, the name: Turn-Key Operation. The franchisee is licensed the right to use the system, learns how to run it, and then "turns the key." The business does the rest. And the franchisees love it! Because if the franchisor has designed the business well, every problem has been thought through. All that's left for the franchisee to do is learn how to manage the system.

Sam Walton separated himself from the crowd by not just building a business but by building a business system that produced results even when he was sleeping.

Abe Marks, the first president of National Mass Retailers' Institute (NMRI) trade association, described Walton's business philosophy:

> He knew that he was already in what the trade calls an "absentee ownership" situation. That just means you're putting your stores out where you, as management, aren't. If he wanted to grow he had to learn to control it. So to service these stores you've got to have timely information: How much merchandise is in the store? What is it? What's selling and what's not? What is to be ordered, marked down, and replaced?

The Information Age has further allowed turnkey operations to blossom because one can study data from each store on a real-time basis. Marks, again, explained why this was crucial for Walton:

> He was really ten years away (in 1966) from the computer world coming. But he was preparing himself. And this is an important point: without the computer, Sam Walton could not have done what he's done. He could not have built a retailing empire the size of what he's built, the way he built it. He's done a lot of other things right, too, but he could not have done it without the computer. It would have been impossible.

Walton studied the data from each store to ensure the targets he set were being hit. In effect, he inspected what he expected. Walton described his process:

> That's why I come in every Saturday morning usually around two or three [a.m], and go through all the weekly numbers. I steal a march on everybody else for the Saturday morning meeting. I can go through those sheets and look at a store, and even though I haven't been there in a while, I can remind myself of something about it, the manager maybe, and then I can remember later that they are doing this much business this week and that their wage cost is such and such. I do this with each store every Saturday morning. It usually takes about three hours, but when I'm done I have as good a feel for what's going on in the company as anybody here—maybe better on some days.

All of this pinpoints one of Walton's key business principles: build a business system that can work anywhere whether the owner is present or not. Billionaire businesses build systems that work without the owner's long-term involvement. For me personally, this was an entirely different way of looking at business and life, for up to that point, I had always focused on how hard I could work rather than how good of a system I could develop. Interestingly, I had been formally trained as a systems engineer, but I had never thought to apply the concept to my personal financial life!

Today, the Internet has leveled the business playing field. Anyone with an entrepreneurial spirit can start a business, building people and a turnkey business system from home. Moreover, people can track their progress by studying real-time data from their home computer.

Billionaires build leaders to orchestrate duplicatable systems to accomplish work. In contrast, the majority of people do not build themselves or systems; thus, they *are* the system that is worked. Indeed, Walton's leadership culture and turnkey business systems were so effective that the business didn't miss a beat after his death. This was possible because he created a business asset that included a top-notch leadership team and a top-notch system.

These are the essential minimums to succeed in building a business asset that outlasts your efforts. Walton's example inspired me to do the same, namely, build leaders and build systems that would work whether I was working that day or not. Now that I understood Buffett's and Walton's key principles of success, I was ready for the third key lesson.

Some debts are fun when you are acquiring them, but none are fun when you set about retiring them.

—OGDEN NASH

CHAPTER 5

ROBERT KIYOSAKI AND THE BILLIONAIRE'S THREE KEYS TO WEALTH

The last piece of the billionaire business success puzzle is from Robert Kiyosaki. He identified three principles that all billionaires apply to produce results. He called them the Three Keys to Wealth:

1. Long-Term Vision
2. Delayed Gratification
3. Utilize the Power of Compounding

These three principles were essential in my financial journey. They led me to study billionaires on my own and see how each one applied the Three Keys to Wealth to his or her particular business. After reading hundreds of business biographies, it became apparent that the principles of success were similar regardless of the specific field in which a person built his or her business asset. Of course, these concepts married wonderfully with what I had learned from Buffett and Walton, and they inspired me to apply my manufacturing systems background to build a business rather than to work a job.

Along the way, I finally understood why Laurie and I were stuck in the Financial Matrix for so long. In effect, we violated every one of the financial principles. We didn't have a long-term financial plan to guide our decision making; we didn't delay our gratification because our emotions consistently trumped our logic; and finally, we had compound interest working against us instead of for us. We knew that when we went to sleep at night, the compound interest wouldn't rest, and we would wake up more broke than we had been the night before. How demoralizing. The Bible says the truth will set you free (John 8:32, NIV), but this is usually the case only after the truth ticks you off. I was ticked, but I was also excited because the plan to escape our Financial Matrix was coming together. Laurie and I committed to making the needed changes. I knew in my heart that the billionaires were no better than us, but they had applied better principles. However, if we did what they did, then we could live as they lived.

> **The Bible says the truth will set you free, but this is usually the case only after the truth ticks you off.**

> **If we did what the billionaires did, then we could live as they lived.**

The Mentors and the Plan

After my business partners and I had studied the key lessons from Buffett, Walton, and Kiyosaki outlined above and studied the financial challenges of people in the civilized world, the LIFE Leadership business plan practically wrote itself. First, LIFE Leadership developed the Financial Fitness

Program (FFP) to help thousands of people reduce debt and stress. Second, since thousands of people were enjoying better financial defense, LIFE Leadership created a plan for offense around investing in personal development and building a business asset. LIFE Leadership has a low-cost personal development plan to build the soft skills in people and a turnkey marketing system to help people build a business asset to share the FFP information with others. We thought: why not create a business asset that helps people learn financial literacy (defense, offense, and playing field of finances) and rewards people for modeling finances and messaging the financial plan to others? LIFE Leadership's compensated community leverages the billionaire's principles (minimize expenses, maximize investments, and build a business asset) to help the 99.9% of the people stuck in the Financial Matrix develop a plan to escape. Already, LIFE Leadership has helped many people escape the Financial Matrix entirely, while many more are on their way to freedom.

Finally, why not compensate people in a fair and equitable manner for spreading the financial message to the world? The monthly compensation can vary for people between a few dollars to tens of thousands of dollars per month, based upon their goals, efforts, and results. Many join the compensated community in order to have an accountability group to keep themselves disciplined to their new financial plan (defense). Others, however, are applying both the defense and the offense by building large and profitable compensated communities. People choose their own commitment level based on the results they desire. Indeed, LIFE Leadership isn't just a business built on purpose; it's actually our purpose built on business. The LIFE Leadership founders apply the principles we teach. We were each stuck in the Financial Matrix just like nearly everyone else. Fortunately, however, through practicing the principles learned from the billionaires and shared in the FFP, the LIFE Leadership founders were able to break free from the Financial Matrix.

After we confirmed we had an accurate roadmap out of the Financial Matrix, the founders created LIFE Leadership to share the roadmap with others. Instead of protesting injustices by occupying streets or attending tea parties (the historical record of peasant protest is extremely poor, anyway), we believe the best way to protest is non-participation in the Financial Matrix, a concept that marries the ideas of personal responsibility and the application of the billionaire principles. Let's call it "conscientious objection"; our consciences object to participating in the Financial Matrix any longer!

This is the core teaching of LIFE Leadership: consistently spend less than you make and invest the difference in yourself (Buffett's two financial secrets). Then build a turnkey business system by sharing the financial principles with others to produce wealth and freedom outside the Financial Matrix.

Now that we understand Buffett's and Walton's principles, it's time to learn how LIFE Leadership applies the billionaire's Three Keys to Wealth (long-term vision, delayed gratification, and the power of compounding) so you can utilize these principles to *live the life you've always wanted.*

Give fools their gold and knaves their power;
Let fortune's bubbles rise and fall;
Who sows a field or trains a flower
Or plants a tree is more than all.

—John Greenleaf Whittier

CHAPTER 6

LONG-TERM VISION

In order to *live the life you've always wanted,* you're probably going to have to face some things you've always avoided. Essentially, a person's circumstances will not change until the person does. This is where long-term vision comes into play. People cannot change their future until they

> In order to *live the life you've always wanted,* you're probably going to have to face some things you've always avoided.

have the courage to envision it. After all, vision is just tomorrow's reality expressed as an idea today. And only when people see the vision in their mind are they capable of bringing it into reality. The vision, in other words, must come before the action. Unfortunately, few people have a long-term financial vision. Instead, most people are like sailboats without a rudder, merely blown in the financial wind. Laurie and I knew that our long-term vision was bigger than just being job-optional. We wanted total independence from the Financial Matrix debt system without having to live like paupers.

In a similar fashion, it is necessary to invest the time to express this long-term vision as an idea today. As my good friend and cofounder of LIFE Leadership Bill Lewis says, "It's not how big you dream; it's how long you dream big." Success, in a sense, is a picture in the mind's eye that you maintain no matter what. What success picture do you have the courage to imagine? Once a person eliminates debt, his or her money begins to accumulate quickly, so he or she should not delay in cultivating a vision for the future. Remember, dreams come true for those who are true to their dreams. The first part of being true to a dream is expressing it verbally because the long-term vision is defining the life a person desires once time and money are no longer constraints. To be sure, achieving dreams demands time and sacrifice, but that is why it's called long-term vision. A person cannot fix in months what one has taken years to mess up. All real change must first begin with a change in *thinking*.

> **Dreams come true for those who are true to their dreams.**

To change our finances, Laurie and I knew we had to change the way we thought about money, time, and wealth creation. This is why Buffett's advice was so important to us. We need not only financial defense (to minimize expenses) but also financial offense (to maximize investments). In today's microwave world, a decade may seem like an eternity, but in reality, time passes quickly. Do you remember where you were when the Twin Towers fell? I certainly do. I received a phone call from my good friend Chris Brady in time to turn on my rarely-used television and watch both towers fall. I was practically in a state of shock. Defining moments like this are rarely forgotten and are remembered vividly as if they happened yesterday. But almost unbelievably, the Twin

Towers collapsed nearly fourteen years ago! Like I said, time flies, regardless of what we do with it along the way.

Realize that a decade is going to go by whether you develop a long-term vision or not. However, your financial results will be much different depending upon the choices you make during that decade. Laurie and I committed to a decade of discipline in order to radically change our finances. Inexorably, the decade has come and gone, but the discipline has changed everything. We applied the Three Keys to Wealth consistently, and by late 2003 (almost ten years to the day later), we paid off the mortgage on our 8,300-square-foot home. We were officially free from the Financial Matrix. Better yet, we have not borrowed any money since then. I am not saying this to shed light on us, but rather to shed light on the effectiveness of the principles taught in Financial Fitness Program. The principles work. The only question is whether you will discipline yourself to apply the principles. Thankfully, this is made much easier by associating with others in the LIFE Leadership community who are also applying the defensive and offensive principles consistently in order to break free from the Financial Matrix. As the Bible says, "Iron sharpens iron (Proverbs 27:17, NIV)."

There are several questions to answer in developing a long-term financial vision. First, if you knew your vision couldn't fail, what would it include? Needless to say, your vision should include more than just material things (houses, cars, and toys). It should also involve the type of person you want to become, the type of friends you want to associate with, and the legacy you intend to leave. Your long-term vision, in effect, should be the successful realization of your "tombstone test." This is where you see yourself at your funeral and imagine what people will say about your life and work. Once you know your long-term vision, you can then identify the proper roadmap to take you from your present reality to your future vision.

The Ant and the Elephant

Author Jack Canfield writes that you have control over only three things in life: "the thoughts you think, the images you visualize, and the action you take." Since the conscious mind thinks in words, while the subconscious mind thinks in images, few people realize the subconscious mind is actually much more powerful than the conscious one. Olympian Vince Poscente, for example, termed the two minds "the ant and the elephant." He explained that the conscious (ant) mind stimulates 2,000 neurons per second while the subconscious (elephant) mind stimulates four billion neurons per second. In other words, the subconscious mind is two million times more powerful in programming the brain than is the conscious mind. Researcher Erik Calonius elaborates:

> Scientists are discovering that the brain is a vision-ary device, the primary function of which is to create pictures in our minds that can be used as blueprints for things that don't exist. They are also learning that our brains can work subconsciously to solve problems that we cannot crack through conscious reasoning, and that the brain is a relentless pattern seeker, constantly reinventing the world.

To accomplish a long-term vision, you must learn to program your subconscious mind with positive images of your future life. As Albert Einstein once stated, "Imagination is everything. It is the preview of life's coming attractions."

Please don't misunderstand me; I'm not telling you that sitting on the sofa all day and visualizing your future will mysteriously make all your dreams come true. Rather, as Olympian Peter Vidmar stressed, "Visualization is not a substitute for hard work and dedication. But if you add it to your training regimen—whether in sports, business, or your personal relationships—you will prepare your mind for success, which is the first step in achieving all your goals and dreams." Interestingly, historian Eugene Ferguson described a similar phenomenon when he wrote:

> Pyramids, cathedrals, and rockets exist not because of geometry, theory of structures, or thermodynamics, but because they were first pictures—literally visions—in the minds of those who first conceived them. Usually the significant governing decisions regarding an artisan's or an engineer's design have been made before the artisan picks up tools or the engineer turns to his drawing board."

While most people say they have to see to believe, achievers actually believe to see. Vision, again, is first seeing in the mind and then acting in the world to make the vision a reality. Dr. Maxwell Maltz emphasized, "The goals that the Creative Mechanism seek to achieve are MENTAL IMAGES or mental pictures, which we create by the use of IMAGINATION." Achievers imagine so vividly that it is experienced as real, leading Maltz to conclude, "Clinical psychologists have proven beyond a shadow of a doubt that the human nervous system cannot tell the difference between an actual experience and an experience imagined vividly and in detail." When you understand the power of belief, you are on the verge of moving any mountains standing in your way.

In 1987, for example, a struggling actor who couldn't even afford to pay his bills drove his old Toyota up Mulholland Drive into the Hollywood Hills. As he stared down at the City of Angels, he imagined his future in vivid detail. By feeding his subconscious mind the long-term vision he imagined, this young actor experienced feelings as if they were real even though they were only imagined in his mind. Before he left, he wrote himself a check, dated for Thanksgiving Day, 1995, "for acting services rendered," in the amount of ten million dollars. To practically everyone else, this action would have seemed absurd, for only the upper echelon actors ever made that type of compensation. Jim Carrey's subconscious, however, experienced the event as real, and years later it *was* real. In fact, Jim Carrey has surpassed twenty million dollars for acting services rendered. If anything, he didn't dream big enough! Actor Jim Carrey consistently fed his elephant mind the future he envisioned and accomplished what author Claude Bristol describes: "This subtle force of repeated suggestion overcomes our reason. It acts directly on our emotions and our feelings, and finally penetrates to the very depths of our subconscious minds. It's the repeated suggestion that makes you believe."

Action: Where the Rubber Meets the Road

Now that we have the vision right, it's time to get the actions right. Financial success demands excellent defense and offense to outrun the Financial Matrix. Success is hard work, but failure is hard also and lasts longer. As part of LIFE Leadership's turnkey marketing system, we studied many people who successfully escaped the Financial Matrix to determine what behaviors they practiced in common. The behaviors fell into four main areas:

- Reading
- Listening
- Associating
- Applying

These four practices help people move from an employee/self-employed mindset to a turnkey business owner mindset. For that reason, LIFE Leadership created the Power Player program to help people combine the right process with the right actions. The Power Player program combines each of these four steps into an organized program that is both fun and rewarding to follow. Such a program makes it easier to acquire the new habits necessary for success that often come disguised simply as hard work. Indeed, hard work combined with a few improvements (through mentorship and studying other successful people) compounded over 10,000 hours helps people develop mastery.

Interestingly, most people believe mastery is a matter of talent rather than discipline, but researcher K. Anders Ericsson proved otherwise. Indeed, he chose a field that has traditionally been assumed to be filled with naturally talented individuals, the music industry. Certainly, if any field could prove that hard work alone cannot produce mastery, it would be the musical profession. However, author Malcolm Gladwell described how Ericsson's study proved the exact opposite. The striking thing about Ericsson's study is that he and his colleagues couldn't find any "naturals," musicians who floated effortlessly to the top while practicing a fraction of the time their peers did. Nor could they find any "grinds," people who worked harder than everyone else yet just didn't have what it took to break into the top ranks. Their research suggests that once a musician has enough ability to get into a top music school, the thing that distinguishes one performer from another is how hard he or she works. That's it. And what's more, the people at the very top don't just work harder or even much harder than everyone else. They work much, much harder.

Mastery, as the research has proven, has little to do with talent. Practically everyone has enough talent, but few seem willing to do the hard work combined with the daily improvements compounded over 10,000 hours. I was excited when I read Ericsson's research because I never felt I had much talent, but I knew I could work hard and do so consistently. Still, it isn't just 10,000 hours, for many have worked the hours without achieving mastery. Rather, it's 10,000 hours with proper coaching and course-correcting. Otherwise, someone may believe he or she has 10,000 hours of experience when he or she actually has an hour's experience repeated 10,000 times. Author Geoff Colvin called this constant improvement mindset "deliberate practice" and wrote:

> Deliberate practice is characterized by several elements, each worth examining. It is activity designed specifically to improve performance, often with a teacher's help; it can be repeated a lot; feedback on results is continuously available; it's highly demanding mentally, whether the activity is purely intellectual, such as chess or business-related activities, or heavily physical, such as sports; and it isn't much fun.

Deliberate practice, in effect, separates the amateurs from the professionals in every field. Amateurs typically practice in their comfort zone on skills they have already mastered, while professional work in the uncomfortable zone to expand their range of skill mastery. Abraham Lincoln modeled this attitude when he said, "I will work, I will study, and when my moment comes, I will be ready."

Anyone can master the skills of wealth building, but unless a person is locked into his or her long-term vision, he or she will not persist in the uncomfortable zone to develop mastery. Achievers, in a sense, learn to become comfortable being uncomfortable. This is what is needed for mastery. Perhaps Professor Robert Grudin described it best:

> The process of achieving their professional level is usually full of pain. Such mastery demands endless practice of technical operations, endless assaults on seemingly ineluctable concepts, humiliation by teachers, anxious and exhausting competition with peers. To gain such mastery, one must face the sting of pertinent criticism, the shock of a thousand minor failures, and the nagging fear of one's own un-improvable inadequacy.

So why do achievers do it? Because they hate losing enough to change, while the rest hate changing enough to lose. Achievers endure the pain to receive the gain, while non-achievers skip the pain and the gain. Movie star Will Smith stressed his work ethic when he stated:

Achievers hate losing enough to change, while the rest hate changing enough to lose.

I'm not afraid to die on a treadmill. I will not be out-worked. You may be more talented than me. You might be smarter than me. And you may be better looking than me. But if we get on a treadmill together you are going to get off first or I'm going to die. It's really that simple. I'm not going to be outworked.

Long-term vision, in sum, leads to hard work, which leads to persistence. As Vince Lombardi once proclaimed, "The harder you work, the harder it is to surrender."

Quitters, Campers, and Climbers

When faced with the reality of the Financial Matrix, most people choose to become one of three things, as described by Dr. Paul Stoltz: quitters, campers, or climbers. Quitters feel the pain and exit the game of life by relying upon some escape mechanism to avoid the pain of reality. Quitters become a drain upon society, since they rely upon others to support their needs. Campers, on the other hand, may understand they are trapped in the Financial Matrix, but they refuse to do the work necessary to free themselves. Instead, they seek as much comfort as is possible in the modern matrix of control. Climbers, in contrast, reject the control inherent within the Financial Matrix and yearn to be free. They are not looking for "easy" but only for "worth it." Climbers refuse to settle for good when they know great is available. Furthermore, they believe that since others have made it out of the Financial Matrix, they can too by following the same billionaire principles.

What separates quitters, campers, and climbers is *vision persistence*. Climbers persist until the long-term vision is accomplished, while quitters and campers, by taking their eyes off the prize, can only see the obstacles. At some point on the journey, every quitter and camper has compromised his or her convictions for conveniences. Laurie and I committed to never settle for life inside the Financial Matrix, especially when we knew we now had a financial roadmap (defense and offense) to our freedom.

Tim and Amy Marks: Long-Term Vision

Tim and Amy Marks were hurting. Tim's million-dollar (at least on paper) real estate empire, built through the accumulation of dozens of mortgages, had capsized. Although Tim had been featured as successful on one of the real estate mogul's television ads, a series of calamities (renter defaults, service manager embezzlement, and higher maintenance costs) had his business on the ropes. With a negative cash flow, marriage challenges, and sixteen-hour days split between his supervisor job and managing his real estate properties, it was a terrible time to start another business. Nevertheless, Tim and Amy built the fastest million-dollar business asset of anyone Laurie and I have ever mentored.

How did they do it? While no one worked any harder and they certainly read, listened, and associated to learn the principles quickly, I believe the number one reason they succeeded was because they began with the end in mind. Rarely will someone break out of the Financial Matrix in thirty-one months, but this is exactly what the Marks did. Despite massive financial and emotional stress, they kept their eyes on the prize of debt-free financial freedom. They filled their subconscious

> **Most people sell their dreams to buy their excuses, but those who have long-term vision sell their excuses to buy their dreams.**

minds with the future they desired and didn't let their current reality overcome their future vision.

This is the secret of starting with a long-term vision. Unfortunately, most people sell their dreams to buy their excuses, but those who have long-term vision sell their excuses to buy their dreams. Tim and Amy had plenty of excuses, but they used them as *reasons for* building a business asset. Today, they live in a beautiful home in their dream location of Cape Coral, Florida, have four wonderful children, and are leaders of other leaders along with being cofounders of LIFE Leadership. They are truly a testament to the power of vision persistence!

This would be a much better world if more married couples were as deeply in love as they are in debt.

—EARL WILSON

CHAPTER 7

DELAYED GRATIFICATION

Once you have long-term vision, you are ready to implement the second principle every billionaire practices: delayed gratification. Delayed gratification is the ability to resist an immediate smaller reward and wait instead for a larger, more enduring reward. While most acknowledge this to be a good principle, few seem to live it. The reason why becomes clear when one remembers that marketers and advertisers receive big money to get people to buy on impulse rather than on reason. This returns us to the discussion on the conscious (ant) mind and the subconscious (elephant) mind. In order to delay gratification, you must be programming the elephant subconscious with the long-term vision you desire. Without this vision, however, the marketers will have a field day filling the void with their visions instead. They are experts at harnessing your mental elephant and getting it to charge off in a destructive direction! Therefore, the real question becomes:

> **Delayed gratification is the ability to resist an immediate smaller reward and wait instead for a larger, more enduring reward.**

Who is programming your elephant subconscious? Based upon the lack of delayed gratification across society, for most people, it is apparent that it isn't themselves.

The average person consumes around four to five hours of television and media per day. Therefore, the subconscious mind of most people is deluged with images designed to get them to emotionally buy what they cannot afford. Author Erik Calonius noted the impact such repeated image exposures have on the mind: "The researchers found that the subjects like the pictures they had already seen. Researchers call this the 'mere exposure effect.' That's why advertisers pound ads repeatedly down our throats. It's why chain restaurants (you get the same meal coast to coast) thrive."

Not surprisingly, successful advertisers ignore the conscious (ant) mind and, instead, create an (elephant) charge by feeding the subconscious a steady diet of seductive images. Advertisers have learned from experience that providing a list of functions, features, and benefits to the ant mind doesn't produce results, but feeding alluring images to the elephant mind does. Philosopher Dan Dennett describes the subconscious mind as the "President," while the conscious mind is just its "Press Secretary." As a result, advertisers encourage the "President" to buy things on emotion that people truly don't need, and the "Press Secretary" creates a rational reason to explain the purchases after the fact. Advertisers, in the main, fill imaginations with images of their own making to elicit a buying response that is not wise.

If advertisers can program our subconscious minds to tempt us into the Financial Matrix, then doesn't it make sense that the path out of the Financial Matrix requires that we program our *own* minds? Once I understood that the elephant mind merely charges toward the images it is consistently fed,

Laurie and I began filtering what was fed to our elephant minds. Indeed, this is one of the keys to freedom from the Financial Matrix: refusing to be seduced into buying things we cannot afford. Once people assume responsibility for feeding their elephant mind, they are moving toward their long-term vision. As Dr. Maxwell Maltz explains, "We act, or fail to act, not because of the *will*, as is so commonly believed, but because of imagination. A human being always acts and feels and performs in accordance with what he imagines to be true about himself and his environment."

The book of Luke has a verse that reads, "He that is faithful in that which is least is faithful also in much: and he that is unjust in the least is unjust also in much (Luke 16:10, KJV)." The Financial Fitness Program (FFP) teaches people how to be faithful in their current income, so that they have seed money to invest in themselves and their future. Essentially, if people cannot manage their current income, they will prove unfaithful even when or if they make more. For instance, how many stories have we heard about how lottery winners made and lost millions of dollars, eventually being forced to declare bankruptcy? How is this possible? Simply stated, without a solid financial education, making more money can be dangerous. Indeed, banks and credit cards provide more credit to people with higher incomes, basically providing the rope for financially illiterate people to hang themselves. Thankfully, regardless of how people make their money, the FFP teaches specific defensive principles to help them spend less than they make every month. Playing defense, in other words, is essential to restoring financial liberty. For only when people enjoy financial freedom by making money through their business asset, without having to borrow money, are they truly free from the Financial Matrix.

Robert Kiyosaki created the CASHFLOW Quadrant to identify and explain the four ways people can choose to generate cash flow. Each of the four Quadrants represent a category of income generation: Employee, Self-Employed, B-Business Owner, and Investor. Each of them has pros and cons that must be considered when choosing which Quadrant to work within. Every reader is in one, or more, of these Quadrants, and it's important to understand how to move from one's current Quadrant into the Business and Investor Quadrants in order to escape the Financial Matrix. In truth, it doesn't matter which Quadrant people start in so long as they have long-term vision, delays gratification, and utilize the power of compounding to ultimately move themselves into the Business and Investor Quadrants.

The important principle is to live below your current income to generate the seed money to invest in your business asset and harvest your financial freedom.

Employee Quadrant: "Per Hour" Pros and Cons

Repeat after me. If you want to be successful, you need to get good grades, get a good job with benefits, and then you can live the American Dream. Anyone ever hear that one growing up? I heard that hundreds of times growing up. A good job, in reality, does provide a high level of security (at least in a good economy) since an employee receives income whether he or she, or the company, were productive that month. Employees, in short, get paid per hour sold. This leads to predictable levels of income and an easier path with which to develop a solid defensive financial plan. If, however, a person's income varies month to month, it becomes difficult to build an effective defensive plan. Above everything else is the little downside risk if the company fails. In this case, an employee merely gets another job, while the entrepreneur who started a traditional brick-and-mortar business is typically still responsible for paying creditors back. Indeed, if the business owner cannot handle the debt load, he or she will end up in bankruptcy proceedings. The Employee Quadrant, in sum, is a great short-term place for people to start their journey to the Business and Investor Quadrants since it provides a steady stream of income. The predictable income allows people to live below their means and to invest the difference into building a business to free themselves from the Financial Matrix.

However, employees who choose to remain employees must also recognize the risk associated with this choice. First, for any people who consider themselves to be hungry, hone-able, and honorable, the upside rewards in a job environment are minimal. Pay raises are typically distributed within a small range regardless of each individual's personal contribution. At most, a high achiever may make 5–10% more than the average even though he or she may be contributing ten times more to the company's bottom line. Long-term employees, in essence, follow a forty-five-year plan in which incomes level off around twenty-five years of age, and raises barely keep up with the cost of living afterward. This flat line continues until retirement, when the employees are then forced to make it on 50% or less of the income they already thought wasn't enough when they were working full-time.

Interestingly, when I learned about the Employee Forty-Five-Year Plan, I was twenty-six years old. I remember sitting down with my dad to graph it out for him. I showed him how employee pay flatlined from around age twenty-five until age sixty-five and told him this wasn't working for me. His response, as a sixty-year-old retired electrician, was classic: "You know what son? It didn't work for me either! I'm making less than half in retirement of what I made working full-time." While this is funny today, it wasn't when I first heard it! I had spent eight years of my life climbing a ladder that could not take me where I wanted to go. If the definition of insanity is continuing to do the same thing while expecting a different result, then I was flirting with the edge of insanity.

The 45 Year Plan

AGE - years

Source: U.S. Dept of Labor

Above all, however, the final straw that leads people out of the E-Quadrant is when employees realize they are at the mercy of the company's leadership for their security and advancement. For example, when I resigned from AC Rochester to start my own consulting company, many told me it was risky. Nevertheless, I felt it was riskier to rely on the company's management bureaucracy for my economic future rather than on my own performance. In particular, if the management team made poor decisions, they affected everyone else regardless of their personal achievements. Further, because growth had slowed in our division, I was told at twenty-five years old that there were over 100 too many eighth levels (a much sought-after level of distinction within the enormous General Motors hierarchy) already and that they could not consider promoting me again until I was at least thirty-two years old. Seven years of working hard to hopefully get promoted seemed silly to me. Unfortunately, to many others it didn't. After AC Rochester became independent of GM, it tanked in a few short years. In the aftermath, tens of thousands of employees (both salaried and hourly) lost their jobs regardless of their personal performance. This, in sum, is the danger of remaining an employee long-term.

Self-Employed Quadrant: "Per Task" Pros and Cons

Self-employed people are usually those who recognized the downside risk associated with the E-Quadrant and did something about it. This is courageous, and S-Quadrant income earners ought to be commended for making the entrepreneurial leap. A large benefit of a self-employed business situation is the greater level of control people have over their business and income potential. Self-employed people launch a business based upon their specific skills to satisfy customers in the marketplace. Many S-Quadrant people (like private practice doctors, lawyers, accountants) get paid per service or task. This typically allows them to make more money and have more control over their futures than employees have. Control is important to the S-Quadrant inhabitants, as most of them started a company because they felt more secure controlling their own destiny rather than relying upon others. Indeed, that is precisely why I left AC Rochester and started my own engineering consulting company. I leveraged the recognition I had received from winning a National Technical Benchmarking Award and the skills I learned through technical benchmarking at AC Rochester to move from the

E- to the S-Quadrant. I felt more secure in my own ability to perform and believed I could build an S-Business around teaching the benchmarking process to other companies. The next thing I knew, I was traveling around the country building my own self-employed business model making more money per hour than I ever had before.

Unfortunately, while there are many upsides in the S-Quadrant, there are also some downsides. For one thing, I discovered that building a big consulting company meant being willing to travel around the globe. However, with four young children at home at the time, I wasn't excited about this necessity. For another, I realized that in order to make money, I still had to directly contribute my time. I had merely traded a dollars-per-hour job for a dollars-per-service self-employed business. Regardless of how ambitious I was, I was still caught in the money-for-time trap. Considering what Kiyosaki once said: "Never invest in a business where the system goes home at night", I realized that I was the system that went home at night! In other words, the business could only get as big as the swapping of my time, and this limited the success of my (and every other) S-Business.

Finally, I found that in the S-Quadrant, I went from having one boss (as an employee) to having numerous bosses (customers) with conflicting agendas. In effect, it became increasingly difficult to satisfy all my customers, and I knew it would only get worse the bigger my business grew. In a sense, moving from the E-Quadrant to the S-Quadrant was like jumping from the frying pan into the fire. True, I made more money, but I also increased my time, travel, and responsibilities with no end in sight. S-Business owners are like barge operators who make money by carrying cars across a river. While they can make good money, they are limited by how many trips they are willing and able to drive the barge from one side to the other. Curiously, even though I told everyone I owned my own business, I soon realized the business actually owned me.

Business Owner Quadrant: "Per Relationship" Pros and Cons

The breakthrough for me personally occurred when I began studying B-Business owners and discovered they made money based upon the value of their business asset. If an S-Business owner is like a barge owner, then a B-Business owner is someone who builds a bridge instead. With a bridge, the cars can transport themselves across the river by paying a toll to use the business asset created by the B-Business owner.

The benefits of building a B-Business were easy to identify: the business works even when you don't. With routine maintenance on the bridge, the tolls accrue daily in an income stream not directly tied to how many hours or how many tasks one performs. In essence, the business system does not go home at night.

I remember hearing Michael Dell give a talk to the Detroit Economic Club when he was worth around $21.5 billion, even though he was only several years older than I was. Needless to say, my net worth at the time was slightly under $21.5 billion (maybe $21.499 billion short or so!), and I couldn't understand how Dell could achieve more than all the salaries of all the engineers I worked with. Even if Dell were five times smarter and worked twice as hard (he couldn't work any harder since I routinely put in twelve-hour days), then he should have been around ten times wealthier than I was, not millions of times wealthier! This helped me see the difference between the E- and S-Quadrants, which trade time for money, and the B-Quadrant, which builds leaders and systems to create a business asset that generates ongoing income.

I finally understood why the key to escaping the Financial Matrix is to build a business asset. Since the asset is what makes money rather than a person, the asset can work indefinitely without getting tired or needing sleep. Hence, the bigger the business gets, the more it frees a person financially from the time/money trap. I knew I would be stuck in the Financial Matrix for decades unless I learned to build people and systems as had Sam Walton and the other successful B-Quadrant businesses owners. The systems side wasn't a problem, as I was a manufacturing systems engineer. However, the people side was not going to be easy for this poor-people-skills engineer strong in high-tech and weak in high-touch skills. Later, I would learn that assembling a leadership team and the long-term relationships cultivated in doing so would bring some of the greatest joy. At first, however, the thought of working with people only produced fear and trepidation. Nonetheless, if the path to freedom demanded we develop a business asset that generated ongoing income through building people and systems, then that is what Laurie and I would do. I wasn't exactly sure how we would do this, but I promised to do whatever it would take (legally, morally, and ethically) to make it happen.

Of course, the downside of a B-Business is that it requires effort to develop a leadership and systems mindset and at the same time offers no guarantees of success. Some would see this as risky, but I viewed it as a great challenge. One of my first mentors taught me, "When the going gets tough, the tough get

> **The key to escaping the Financial Matrix is to build a business asset.**

going." I used this saying many times in my life to get going when things were tough. Eventually I developed my own saying: "You either hate losing enough to change or you hate changing enough to lose." I didn't necessarily like change, but I HATED losing, and I knew I had to make the leap from the E- and S-Quadrants to the B-Quadrant (and to some degree the I-Quadrant). To do so, I would need new information because the thinking that had produced my existing results had been learned from my E and S mentors. I knew to make new decisions, I would need new information, so I started a daily regimen of reading personal development books and listening to audios to make myself into the leader capable of succeeding in a B-Quadrant business.

Investor Quadrant: "Per ROI" Pros and Cons

The I-Quadrant consists of investors who are free from the Financial Matrix through applying consistent defense and offense to their finances. The financially free investors have wiped out all their debts (including home mortgages) and have built investments producing enough income to enable them to live indefinitely outside of the Financial Matrix. In other words, they are debt-free and cash-rich, and they receive enough residual incomes to live financially free. This should be the long-term goal of every person in the civilized world.

The I-Quadrant investors have applied long-term vision and delayed gratification and now enjoy the power of compounding in their favor. Indeed, when debt-free B- or I-Quadrant people go to bed at night, they wake up wealthier—a sure sign that they have broken free from the Financial Matrix. Investors now have money making money for them. And, when their I-Quadrant income is enough to support their lifestyle, they can live indefinitely without income from the E-,

S-, and even the B-Quadrants. Whereas every other quadrant invests time to make money (even the B-Quadrant sells time to build people and systems), the I-Quadrant is the only one that invests money to make money and thus buys back time.

Naturally, the I-Quadrant upside is the money, time, and freedom from the Financial Matrix, while the downside is simply the time and effort invested to reach it. My thought, however, was that it takes effort no matter which quadrants one works in; therefore, we may as well apply the effort to first build a B-Business to free us from the time-for-dollars trap and then eventually reach the I-Quadrant, where money can make money for us. Indeed, an employee, a self-employed person, or a B-Business owner can all reach the I-Quadrant and escape the Financial Matrix, but the fastest route is to leverage the left-side Quadrants for the short-term security and the right-side Quadrants for the long-term vision. Let me say that again: The fastest route for most is to leverage the left-side Quadrants for the short-term security and the right-side Quadrants for the long-term vision fulfillment.

> **The fastest route to escape the Financial Matrix is to leverage the left-side Quadrants for the short-term security and the right-side Quadrants for the long-term vision.**

The long-term vision for Laurie and me was freedom from the Financial Matrix over the next decade. We set this goal in late 1993. By late 2003, we had paid off the mortgage, and we have lived debt-free ever since. Over the last couple of years, our investments alone have returned enough to support our lifestyle. Ultimately, life in the I-Quadrant is available to anyone willing to apply the same principles consistently.

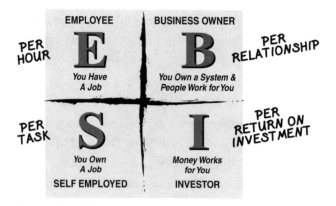

Robert Kiyosaki's CASHFLOW Quadrant

Dan and Lisa Hawkins' Story

Dan and Lisa Hawkins (to use just one of the LIFE Leadership founders as an illustration) are an excellent example of a young couple who took Warren Buffett's advice to heart. When they studied the principles in the Financial Fitness Program, they realized their lack of capital was hindering their ability to go on offense. To use a football analogy, their defense was so poor that their offense rarely stepped onto the field. Through mentorship, however, Dan and Lisa got serious about debt reduction. Although they only made fifty thousand dollars per year combined, they quickly wiped debt out by applying the proper financial principles. For instance, Dan was spending eight to ten dollars every day on vending machine snacks and drinks and an additional five to ten dollars on lunch. These expenses were quickly cut out as Dan began packing a lunch from home and curtailing his soda pop consumption on the job. They also canceled their cable subscription, began to read more, and used the money they normally spent on movies and dinners out for business training and personal development materials instead.

Gaining confidence in practicing delayed gratification, Dan sold his hotrod Mustang and paid cash for a $3,000 replacement vehicle. He then used the remaining cash to pay off Lisa's car, effectively eliminating $600 of monthly payments. With the extra monthly cash flow, Dan and Lisa paid off one credit card and then another, and over a couple of years, they eliminated two car loans, several credit card balances, an ATV loan, a computer loan, student loans, and finally their mortgage!

Dan and Lisa disciplined themselves to follow four simple principles, which are among the forty-seven principles taught in the defense, offense, and playing field of the Financial Fitness Program:

1. When you receive income, immediately put 10% toward savings.
2. Then, minimize expenses (self-entertainment) and maximize investments (self-education).
3. Service all debts with minimum payments except the highest interest rate debt, which should be paid down with all extra funds.
4. After the first three items are done, pay the rest of the bills.

Once the process was rolling, the victories being achieved created momentum for future successful outcomes. Not surprisingly, thanks to their disciplined approach to finances, the Hawkins family eventually accumulated thousands of dollars in savings. With their business income continuing to grow and all debt eliminated, their nest egg grew rapidly. This allowed them the freedom to purchase a house three times as big as their previous one with a substantial down payment. As Dan and Lisa built up their savings, they retired debt and used the larger cash flow to increase investment in themselves and their growing business. Newer cars and better vacations followed as the Hawkins family lived a cash lifestyle in which they only spent money they had already earned. Still, they kept saving a portion of all income. Amazingly, through increases in their business and consistent financial discipline, the Hawkins family went on to buy an 8,500-square-foot custom home on over twenty acres, paying almost 50% (goal is to pay off mortgage within five years) equity at closing. Dreams do come true for those who read, listen to, learn, and apply the timeless principles of financial fitness.

Today, Dan and Lisa lead a multimillion-dollar leadership company and speak around North America teaching financial and leadership principles to others. By following Buffett's two key wealth-building principles of getting out of debt and investing in themselves, Dan and Lisa Hawkins went from living in dread to living their dreams.

The man who never has money enough to pay his debts has too much of something else.

—JAMES LENDALL BASFORD

CHAPTER 8

UTILIZE THE POWER OF COMPOUNDING

Now that we have implemented a long-term vision for the future (to break free from the Financial Matrix) and are using this long-term vision to practice delayed gratification (playing defense), we are ready to go on offense by utilizing the power of compounding.

Before we get into the details of offense, let me ask you a question. If I owned Microsoft and offered to sell it to you for $100, would you buy it? How about Exxon Mobil Corporation for $100? Finally, if I offered you Chipotle Mexican Grill for $100, would you be in? If you are anything like me, you would enthusiastically agree to all three bargains, even if you don't have any expertise or experience in the three businesses. Why? Because you, just like me, don't care what business it is so long as it works (and is legal, moral, and ethical).[4]

Business author Michael Gerber taught similarly when he explained that the key to a turnkey business system has "less to do with what's done in a business and more to do with how it's done. The commodity isn't what's important—the way it's delivered is." In a similar fashion, LIFE Leadership has created a turnkey marketing system for people to plug into and apply, and with time, the combination of defense and offense helps them escape the Financial Matrix by building a business asset.

Needless to say, in order to build a business asset and obtain financial freedom, one must move from the left side of the CASHFLOW Quadrant to the right side. However, quitting one's job or S-Business is risky and not feasible for most people. Thus, the best plan to escape the Financial Matrix includes working on the left side of the Quadrant while building leaders and a turnkey system on the right side. This plan provides security, through maintaining one's current job or self-employed business while also providing opportunity through building a B-Business after work hours. Entrepreneurial risk, in other words, can be greatly reduced by leveraging the security of one side of the Quadrant while striving for the independence offered by the other side.

In particular, Laurie and I were looking for a business that leveraged the latest technologies and strategies to give ourselves the best opportunity to succeed in our own B-Business. When the cofounders created LIFE Leadership, we did so by tying into four important world trends:

- Home-Based Businesses
- the Internet
- Distribution
- Franchising

Home-Based Business (HBB)

A home-based business (HBB) was a necessity since Laurie and I didn't have the financial wherewithal to invest in a bricks-and-mortar company. Indeed, the cost of rent, inventory, and employees takes most of a start-up's revenue and leaves it on the edge of fiscal solvency. We knew our financial situation was tenuous enough without the additional expenses associated with a traditional business. The goal was to get out of debt, not go further into it, and only an HBB model provided us with the opportunity to win or lose based upon our efforts.

Moreover, there are legal tax deductions available to people who are building a home business that are not accessible to employees. An HBB, in other words, permits the owner to write off legitimate business expenses while keeping overall expenses low by using the home and other assets he or she regularly utilizes anyway. This trend has leveled the entrepreneurial playing field and allows people to compete with hunger rather than with capital. Laurie and I may have lacked capital, but we made up for it with our hunger and the benefits of building our business from home. I worked at a job during the day to pay our bills, Laurie stayed at home to raise our family, and we both worked our HBB at night to achieve our dreams.

The Internet

There has never been a better time to start a home-based business because the Internet has changed the rules of the game. Indeed, the "bricks-versus-clicks" revolution has made it possible for people to build a business from their home that generates more revenue than the largest Wal-Mart store. Furthermore, by leveraging the Internet, an HBB can do this for a fraction of the cost of a traditional retail store. The Internet allows people to offer products around the world from their home without having to have inventory tied up in each state, province, or country. This is a huge competitive advantage for small entrepreneurs over large corporations. Interestingly, although most people understand the Internet has changed the rules of the game and they have even purchased some products online, few have learned how to create a profitable online business. Consequently, when people combine the benefits of an Internet model and an HBB, they have the benefits of left-side Quadrant security with right-side Quadrant opportunity (low cost, low risk, and high profit potential). This is the safest formula to follow for people who want to make the entrepreneurial leap to escape the Financial Matrix.

Distribution

A typical distribution chain starts with the manufacturer, who then sells the product to the national wholesaler, who then moves it to the regional wholesaler, who then sells it to the store, which sells the product to the customer. This five-step distribution process is highly inefficient, especially in the Internet Age. In contrast, an online manufacturer can make a product and then sell it directly to its customers from its own website. This improved distribution system cuts out at least three levels of middle-man profits which add nothing to the product except higher costs and prices. Moreover, manufacturers no longer need massive inventories, since many of the products can be built after the order is placed and shipped directly to the end consumer.

When the benefits of an efficient distribution system are combined with the competitive advantages associated with an Internet-based home business, it becomes much easier to see light at the end of the financial tunnel.

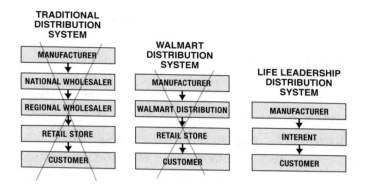

Franchising Model

Finally, the most successful businesses in the world follow a business format franchise model. Companies like McDonald's, Starbucks, and Jiffy Lube, to name just a few, have each built a predictable process to satisfy customers' needs. Few people have built a successful business; therefore, the turnkey system, designed by those who have the experience and results, is leveraged to allow average people to produce un-average results. Michael Gerber explained how Ray Kroc, the pioneering genius of the turnkey business system, developed the original McDonald's system:

> Given the failure rate of most small businesses, he must have realized a crucial fact: for McDonald's to be a predictable success, the business would have to work, because the franchisee, left to his own devices, most assuredly wouldn't! Once he understood this, Ray Kroc's problem became his opportunity. Forced to create a business that worked in order to sell it, he also created a business that would work once it was sold, no matter who bought it. Armed with that realization, he set about the task of creating a foolproof,

predictable business. A systems-dependent business, not a people-dependent business. A business that would work without him.

In the same way, LIFE Leadership set out to create a turnkey marketing system that would work for anyone who did the work of leveraging it. In other words, the entrepreneur does not have to be smart enough or work and invest in order to create the system, but he or she does have to be smart enough and work to leverage it. LIFE Leadership focuses on fulfilling Warren Buffett's two key points for financial success (you'll remember this by now!), eliminating debt at all costs (defense) and investing in self-education (offense). By tapping into LIFE Leadership's number one selling product, the Financial Fitness Program, people will learn the principles of financial defense, offense, and the playing field (the Financial Matrix). Furthermore, LIFE Leadership has created a turnkey business operation that allows people to work on the left side of the Quadrant to eliminate debt and then invest some of the savings to build a right-side Quadrant B-Business. At the same time, people will develop themselves and others by leveraging the turnkey LIFE Training Marketing System.

LIFE Leadership is the best of both worlds because it teaches people to leverage the defense and security of the left side and the offense and freedom of the right side to produce the desired results. With time and effort, people can generate enough money in their B-Business to exit the left side entirely and enjoy their business asset while building I-Quadrant investment income. This is the path to freedom from the Financial Matrix.

The 3 Cs for Successful Internet Companies

You'll remember the day I went to hear Michael Dell speak. Early in the talk, Dell stated that any business that didn't get online within the next couple of years would be out of business. He used a model he called "Direct from Dell," a catalogue ordering system that cut out middlemen even before the Internet was commercially available. As a result, he was one of the earliest online adopters. Later in his talk he listed the "3 Cs" necessary to succeed online:

- Content
- Commerce
- Community

Content

The content side of an Internet business is the website and the products available. As I've stated before, LIFE Leadership's top product is the Financial Fitness Program. It teaches people how to play successful defense and live below their means, while also giving them the guidelines and options of how to launch a financial offense. Finally, it teaches customers about the Financial Matrix and the "playing field" they find themselves on. In addition, since Buffett said to invest in self-education, LIFE Leadership provides an entire array of life-changing information in what we call the 8 F categories of life (Finances, Following, Freedom, Fitness, Friends, Faith, Fun, and Family). But since finances seem to be the area in which most people are hurting, LIFE Leadership usually focuses on the financial "F" first in order to help people get some financial breathing room.

Of course, wisdom in all the 8 Fs is part of investing in self-education to recognize the difference between an investment (that leads to a return) and an expense (that consumes money without any return). Earlier, I mentioned one of the keys to success is reading, listening, and associating with others who have accomplished the results one desires. The content of LIFE Leadership materials involves reading, listening, and associating with others who are freeing themselves from the Financial Matrix. The LIFE Leadership website, lifeleadership.com, has an impressive mix of life-changing products available in each of the 8 F categories. Once people learn that borrowing money to entertain themselves only adds stress, they will begin minimizing expenses and maximizing investments in themselves, and LIFE Leadership's portfolio of products is there to help.

Commerce

The commerce piece of an Internet business is how products are produced directly by the manufacturer and delivered directly to the customer without middlemen. This generates an impressive level of savings on marketing expenses, since LIFE Leadership ships its award-winning financial and leadership materials directly to customers. Low inventory and overhead costs along with high-value proposition products separate LIFE Leadership from the rest of the financial and leadership fields. LIFE Leadership then uses the money saved in the commerce steps to reward its members for sharing the life-changing information with others.

Consider this scenario: a person realizes he or she needs to get out of the Financial Matrix, so the person purchases the Financial Fitness Program to learn how to play defense. Once this person realizes that defense alone is a twenty-to-thirty-year plan for most people, he or she may choose to speed up the process by going on offense and building a business asset by becoming a member of LIFE Leadership. At this point, the person leverages the experiences and results of others building their own business asset. In the process, he or she turns a twenty-to-thirty-year plan for freedom into a possible two-to-five-year plan.

Without exaggeration, practically everyone needs what LIFE Leadership offers: improved financial management (defense, which reduces expenses), wealth thinking (investments in self and business assets), and an understanding of the playing field (the Financial Matrix).

Community

The community section, however, is by far the most important because in LIFE Leadership, people are in business for themselves but not by themselves. Each person or couple has a support team to teach them how to apply the defense, offense, and playing field of finances to achieve their dreams.

Dell said back in 1999 that he had not at that time entirely discovered how to create a loyal community, but LIFE Leadership has through compensating its members for recommending its products. LIFE Leadership has created a "Compensated Community" that pays members a bonus based upon sales and volume moved per month. The more sales and volume produced, the more income generated.

Importantly, regardless of when or where a person starts in the community, he or she can achieve a higher compensation than the person who introduced him or her to LIFE Leadership. Since compensation is based on sales and the volume of product flow through the number of communities each person builds, anyone can make the most money based upon his or her leadership and results. Unlike a typical job, where the boss always makes more than those who report to him or her, the performer gets paid the most regardless of where he or she starts in the organization.

Imagine as the community grows, a person begins making part-time what he or she makes at his or her full-time job. Once this happens, the person can quickly wipe out his or her debt by living on his or her job income and paying down debt from his or her newly created business asset. Of course, when a person starts eliminating debt and building a business asset, he or she becomes very loyal to his or her own products, since the person is seeing the results of the new knowledge applied to his or her personal and professional life.

Finally, LIFE Leadership's turnkey business system includes a "Team Approach" to building the first team ("apprenticeship team") together. The best way for a person to learn how to build communities is to have one of the leaders model and message the proper principles and practices. Team Approach is a systematic method to model and message so the amateur apprentice can quickly become a Professional Business Owner (PBO). Building the apprenticeship community isn't just about who you know that might be interested in better financial defense and offense; rather, it's about who a *team* of people know. This means that, working together with a team, you can create much more results than you would be able to accomplish alone.

Claude and Lana Hamilton's Story

Claude and Lana Hamilton met and married while serving in the Canadian Armed Forces. It wasn't long before the Hamiltons realized that the forced separations and low pay were not a good foundation for building a family. Moreover, the

Hamiltons struggled to meet their bills and accumulated tens of thousands of dollars of debt in the Financial Matrix. Fortunately, the Hamiltons refused to stay there. Through applying the principles taught in the Financial Fitness Program, they disciplined themselves to live below their means and invest the difference in their own business asset. Because they drove used cars and lived in a rented house, many of their friends thought they were crazy. The climb out of debt took several years, but the key was the Hamiltons knew it was their only shot. Instead of focusing on their excuses, they focused on their reasons why. They used the financial and time challenges as fuel to drive them forward in building a business asset. Today, the Hamiltons are living their dreams, having built large compensated communities across the United States and Canada as well as having built one of the largest houses in Halifax, Canada. Claude sits on the Policy Council Board as one of the founders of LIFE Leadership, and the Hamiltons are leading many others toward freedom from the Financial Matrix.

Summary

In closing, just as the Northern states created an Underground Railroad to help Physical Matrix slaves escape north to Canada and freedom, LIFE Leadership has become an "Underground Railroad" to help Financial Matrix subjects escape to financial freedom. We created the Financial Fitness Program to teach the defense, offense, and playing field of finances. Further, we created a turnkey business asset for people who choose to share the FFP strategies with others. When they build a Compensated Community and leverage the proven LIFE Training Marketing System, they are building a B-Quadrant business by developing people and leveraging systems.

Now it's up to you.

Just like Neo in the movie *The Matrix*, you have to choose between the red pill and the blue pill set before you. Are you ready to unplug from the Financial Matrix?

In the movie, Neo asks Morpheus why more people aren't searching for the answers about the nature of the Matrix. The answer Morpheus gives Neo applies similarly to the Financial Matrix today (with my additions in brackets):

> The [Financial] Matrix is a system, Neo. That system is our enemy. But when you're inside, you look around. What do you see? Business people, teachers, lawyers, carpenters—the very minds of the people we are trying to save. But until we do, these people are still a part of that system, and that makes them our enemy. You have to understand, most of these people are not ready to be unplugged. And many of them are so inert, so hopelessly dependent on the [debt] system that they will fight to protect it.[5]

As we wrap up our time together, I want to tell you that I am proud of you for finishing this book. So few people ever read a book cover to cover. The ball is now in your court. I have presented the facts on the Financial Matrix and a roadmap out of the system of control. Will you join the Underground Railroad and free yourself from the Financial Matrix or will you fight to protect your debt?

This is one of those rare life-defining moments. I pray you choose wisely.

Frequently Asked Questions

1. Are there legal tax deductions available for people who build a home-based business?

For people building a true business, there are legal tax deductions for things including training expenses, meeting expenses, and business building car mileage. Consult with a business accountant to ensure you are tracking and recording all business expenses properly.

2. What is the difference between a Compensated Community and a pyramid?

Every reputable multilevel marketing organization separates itself from pyramid schemes and scams by ensuring significant sales of its products to outside customers. Impressively, LIFE Leadership has over 40% of its monthly subscriptions going to customers who are not even part of the compensation plan. This is a testament to just how good the leadership materials are; they are in high demand by many outside the compensated community.

Sadly, some people have drawn the conclusion that network marketing is like a lottery, whereby only a few draw the winning ticket, and everyone else loses. In truth, I was one of those people until I took the time to study the numbers myself. Here is my story of how I went from a community building skeptic to building one of the largest leadership compensated communities in North America.

I graduated from GMI-EMI (now Kettering University) as a manufacturing systems engineer. I became an engineer because I have been fascinated by numbers, statistics, and proportions since I was a kid collecting baseball and football cards. In fact, one summer my brother and I developed an entire board game for baseball based upon player stats and using probabilities that I wasn't supposed to learn until halfway through engineering school. In any event, numbers, data, and the proper reading of the scoreboard have been essential components of Laurie's and my success over the years.

For instance, one of the first conundrums I was faced with when I started studying community building was the following statistic (I am not sure if it was even substantiated) that made its way around the profession: "Only 1 out of 100 people actually makes $50,000 or more per year." At first, this sounds terrible. You mean to tell me that if I get started, I only have a 1 out of 100 chance of making it? But these two statements are not saying the same thing, even though on the surface they may appear to be.

Let me explain.

The first statement ("only 1 out of 100 people make $50,000 or more") is a snapshot of the profession based upon the fact that for anyone to reach the top of the bonus compensation chart (in the case of LIFE Leadership, that's 15,000 points of "product volume"), he must build customers and members while helping them gain enough sales volume for him or her to hit this level. Typically, by the time a person hits the top of the chart (whether he or she does it in three months or three years), he or she has around 100 active members (hence, the 1 out of 100 number). In other words, even if 100% of the people made it, they would still make it by bringing in around 100 other active members (the average number that we see who sell the amount of product necessary to add up to 15,000 points), and the 1% who made it at any particular time would still be true.

However, this doesn't mean the other 100 people cannot *also* bring in customers and members who enjoy the life-changing products and do the exact same thing as the person who brought *them* in. And when they do, they will have built a team of (on average) 100 people; thus, the 1 out of 100 number remains.

Now to my point.

Given that the nature of community building involves building a community (how's that for obvious?) and that a leader's goal is to build 100 active people into his or her community who service customers and members, then the "1 out of 100" number tells us nothing of the success or failure of the business. Rather, it simply reports on the size of the community necessary to earn a certain income, as in my example above when I threw out the hypothetical $50,000.

Indeed, the model is hard-wired, or designed, for a leader to service a community of approximately 100 people in order to reach 15,000 points and thereby achieve what we call the Leader level in LIFE Leadership, resulting in the Leader making anywhere from $20,000 to upwards of $50,000 (with the CAB Program included; see the IDS and Compensation Plan Brochure, as individual results will vary). Therefore, the real question a new person should be asking is not the "1 out of 100" snapshot, which merely reports that a Leader must build around 100 people per community, but rather, how fast can one build 100 people into a community?

Let's consider an example from my automotive process engineering days.

Thousands of sub-assemblies that usually consist of hundreds of parts each are required to build one single automobile. These all come together in a complex process called a final assembly line, in which workers and machines install them, usually on a moving platform or hanger, as the work-in-process car moves down the line. At any given moment in time, if a snapshot of the assembly line were taken, the line would have hundreds of unfinished cars frozen in mid-process. From this snapshot, no one in his or her right mind would argue that only 1 out of 100 cars is ever completed or that the chances of that assembly line making a car would be a mere 1 out of 100! This would be absurd reasoning since the other cars are still "in process" and will be completed shortly, if the assembly line is given a chance to continue producing cars, as it is designed to do.

In effect, the nature of the assembly line guarantees that only 1 car will finish per every 100 (in the example above) on the line at any given time because this is the way the process was designed. It is hard-wired or hard-built to do it in just this way.

It is important to understand that community building is a personal development process similar to the assembly line that builds an automobile.

The difference between a successful and an unsuccessful automotive assembly line is not the 1 out of 100, but rather the rate at which cars move from beginning to completion. If one assembly line moves through the process in one hour, while another takes one year, with all other variables being the same, which would you choose? They both have a snapshot of 1 complete car per 100 in process, but one is moving the process along much more efficiently. Engineers cannot improve the 1 out of 100 on an existing line, but they can improve the throughput by increasing the speed at which the automobiles advance through the process.

In the same way, this is exactly what a Leader does in his or her community building organization. He or she cannot improve the 1 out of 100 because that structure is as locked into the design of the pay plan as is the assembly line process for cars (since the average amount of sales volume across large organizations of people seem to result in roughly that ratio). But he or she can improve the effectiveness of the systematic process to help people achieve top levels faster.

Since everything rises and falls on leadership, LIFE Leadership focuses on helping leaders who serve communities of 100 people be rewarded accordingly. The objective is to speed up the leadership growth process by providing world-class events to attend, audios and books to study, and personal mentoring from which to grow. At the same time, it is up to LIFE Leadership to produce world-class products at price points that sell readily in the marketplace.

In most conventional businesses, it takes years and years for a person to achieve an income above $50,000, after expenses. With the new CAB compensation and Power Player Program, LIFE Leadership is empowering those who work hard consistently to achieve these levels in shorter and shorter amounts of time. True, not everyone is willing to work that hard, nor will everyone go that fast, but the leadership of LIFE Leadership is committed to creating a process wherein people can if they are willing to do what it takes. The question for you is: Are you ready, willing, and able?

I am thankful for my engineering background because it helped me sort through the data to understand what was relevant and what was not. Sadly, many people miss the big picture because they think of community building as a lottery with odds rather than a process with results similar to an automobile assembly line. But for those who will enter into the process and stay long enough to complete their leadership journey, success can become just as predictable as a finished car rolling off the end of an assembly line.

> **Sadly, many people miss the big picture because they think of community building as a lottery with odds rather than a process with results similar to an automobile assembly line.**

I have said many times, LIFE Leadership does not promise "easy," only "worth it." As the Chairman of the Board and one of the principal owners of LIFE Leadership, I wish you all the success you are willing earn!

3. What is Fractional-Reserve Banking, and how is it part of the Financial Matrix?

Fractional-Reserve Banking (FRB) is a process whereby a bank takes the deposits into the bank and then reserves a portion of them (usually between 5–20% depending upon the laws that govern it) and loans out the rest. In other words, if every person who deposited money were to ask for it back, they would not be able to get it because the bank has loaned out your money while allegedly still having it available for your use. But how can money be loaned out and still available to the depositor at the same time? Property, in other words, cannot be "owned" by two people at the same time. In an actual loan, the lender understands he does not have control over the money until the debtor's due date, but in FRB, it does not work that way.

Mysteriously, through the fraudulent FRB system, the bank maintains your access to savings while *also* loaning it out to others. The problem, of course, is the FRB system inflates the money supply (how much so depends upon the reserve ratio chosen) by giving two people (both the depositor and the lender) access to the same money. Indeed, through the use of FRB fiat money (money not backed by gold or silver), the elites have flooded the marketplace with bogus exchange values, causing rapid inflation and rampant injustice. The Financial Matrix was birthed through a web of Fractional-Reserve Banking, increasing national debts, and increasing taxes.

Moreover, the crony-capitalistic FRB system sets the low interest rates which create the boom/bust cycle plaguing modern society. And to add insult to injury, once the FRB system fosters the predictable boom/bust cycle, the boom is credited to the ingenious money controllers, while the bust is blamed on free markets. Apparently, it's a loaded game of heads and tails where heads means the elites win and tails means the masses lose! Although economists the caliber of Ricardo, Mises, and Von Hayek have insisted the FRB system is fraudulent and unstable, it survives through the masses' ignorance and the elites' support. Perhaps British monetary reformer, Michael Rowbotham, described the fraudulent nature of the FRB system the best when he wrote:

> The creation and supply of money is now left almost entirely to banks and other lending institutions. Most people imagine that if they borrow from a bank, they are borrowing other people's money. In fact, when

banks and building societies make any loan, they create new money. Money loaned by a bank is not a loan of pre-existent money; money loaned by a bank is additional money created. The stream of money generated by people, businesses and governments constantly borrowing from banks and other lending institutions is relied upon to supply the economy as a whole. Thus the supply of money depends upon people going into debt, and the level of debt within an economy is no more than a measure of the amount of money that has been created.

In effect, today's Financial Matrix relies upon millions of people willingly selling themselves into financial slavery. For when one combines artificially low centrally-controlled interest rates with the FRB system, one has an enticing combination for consumers and entrepreneurs to borrow money into existence. This money creation, however, leads to the inflation, which means, literally, an increase in the money supply. This predictably results in a boom and eventually a bust when inflation raises prices (which always rise as a result of an increased money supply) above a manageable level. At that point, the consumers and entrepreneurs default on the loans they can no longer service, and the bust wipes out value throughout society. These conditions occurred twice during the Greenspan-controlled central banking era (the period of time in which Alan Greenspan was the Chairman of the Federal Reserve Banking System, the institution that sets interest rates, among other things). In both cases, the artificially-controlled low interest rates fueled consumers' appetites for speculation and "easy" profits. The Internet bubble increased the NASDAQ nearly by a factor of five during the boom between 1995 and

2000, but it then proceeded to collapse by over 60% from 2000–2001.

Unfortunately, those who control the money supply seem to be perpetual optimists who go from failure to failure without learning anything. As a result, when the Twin Towers came crashing down in 2001, Greenspan repeated the same policy that had caused the previous boom/bust cycle. This time, however, money poured into the housing markets, and prices shot upwards of 50% in just a few short years. Not shockingly, the mortgage companies sought to maximize profits by helping everyone qualify for a home mortgage, even those who didn't have steady jobs. The increase in mortgages exploded the money supply, which further fueled higher priced houses and mortgages. The housing bubble was blowing up. Predictably, however, when the non-qualified borrowers could not make their mortgage payments, the housing bubble and the money supply both collapsed, and the financial house of cards would have followed them had it not been for government bailouts.

My good friends and cofounders of LIFE Leadership George and Jill Guzzardo experienced the 2008 boom/bust cycle firsthand. They purchased prime real estate in Tuscon, Arizona for over one million dollars. They put more than 20% down and intended to pay the rest over five years. However, the bust collapsed the real estate market, and the land wasn't worth half of its former price. The Guzzardos ended up selling the property and still owing over $600,000 for land they no longer owned. Thankfully, the Guzzardos were wealthy enough (by building a huge business asset) to weather the storm and learn valuable FRB lessons. Unfortunately, most others cannot afford these financial lessons. Indeed, for many people, the purchase of their dream homes resulted in bankruptcy when the housing market predictably deflated. While practically everyone makes money during the boom, most end up losing everything in the bust. Unbelievably, however, when the negative effects of the boom/bust cycle hit, the main group the government protects is the FRB system that created the issue in the first place. In other words, the fractional-reserve banks reap profit during the boom and secure protection during the bust.

Fractional-Reserve Banking, in sum, is a key aspect for profits and control in the Financial Matrix because it is government-sponsored fraudulent activity that allows bankers to make low-interest loans to the government and the people without actually having the money to do so. Loans are created out of thin air as mere digits on a computer screen. However, the productive entrepreneurs and workers must pay back these loans with *real* production dollars. The Financial Matrix is so ubiquitous because it provides *fake* loans to be paid back with interest from real money earned from *real* production. The best strategy against the Financial Matrix is for people to delay their gratification and build their assets so that they can avoid the Financial Matrix by avoiding the loans that entrap them into it.

4. What was the legal dispute between some of the LIFE Leadership leaders, Quixtar, and MonaVie about?

I get asked this question periodically even though the dispute ended way back in 2010. Still, I believe the highlights from the issue can help people understand the principles LIFE Leadership is founded upon. Before discussing the details, however, I think it's important to share that I have no hard feelings for anyone who worked with Quixtar or currently works with Amway. As a matter of fact, I still have friends that work within the company. I believe life is too short to carry grudges and what is past is past. Further, I have heard from several sources that Amway has softened its litigation policy against leaders who want to leave the company. For this, I am thankful. Finally, I learned a ton during my time with Quixtar and had many memorable experiences. As a resut, I have taken the good, flushed the bad, and moved ahead with no animosity.

Before LIFE Leadership was launched, Laurie and I, along with some of the other top leaders, worked with the Quixtar company to build our community (business asset). Quixtar was a North American Internet-based multilevel business started by the owners of Amway but set up as a separate company from its parent. This was an important feature to me because I had joined Amway in 1993 when I learned they were developing an interactive distribution model to combine high-tech and high-touch. Regretfully, however, by 1998, I realized this was more hype than substance and had not come to fruition. Since Laurie and I had no interest in building a traditional Amway business, we planned on starting a new venture.

Nevertheless, after hearing Ken McDonald (Quixtar's first managing director) share his vision for an online model that would be a separate company backed by Amway money, we were intrigued. Accordingly, in 1999, we did not renew our Amway distributorship and joined Quixtar instead as an Independent Business Owner (IBO). The online model fit our young and hungry team perfectly. In fact, from 1999 through 2007, Laurie and I led the fastest growing organization within the company. We grew from several hundred to over ten thousand people attending events, and our sales increased from a couple hundred thousand dollars to over one hundred million dollars! In addition, many other teams sought our training and started growing also, resulting in nearly another hundred million dollars in volume. Our training organization, in other words, was responsible for nearly two hundred million dollars of Quixtar's total sales.

Unfortunately, the rest of Quixtar was not doing well, mainly because the older, more mature organizations seemed unable to adjust to building an online business. I saw the loss of confidence and numbers firsthand because I was asked to speak consistently to Quixtar groups across North America. Dismally, instead of growing into the one-hundred-billion-dollar company Ken McDonald and other top leaders envisioned, Quixtar leveled off around a billion dollars (even with our team's meteoric growth). In fact, many of the top leaders lost half their numbers or more as they struggled to marry high-touch communities with the high-tech online environment. Nonetheless, I didn't realize the precarious nature of the Quixtar business until Ken McDonald abruptly announced his retirement in 2005, despite having flown to see me just weeks earlier to discuss future strategies. To say I was disappointed would be an understatement (Ken and I worked well together), but I also respected Quixtar's right to choose its leadership team.

Curiously, however, Quixtar's new managing director was also an Amway vice-president. Although I thought this was strange, I was assured on numerous occasions that the two were still separate corporations and the change in management was merely to help Quixtar increase its sales. As a result, the 2007 announcement that Quixtar was closing its doors and that all its Independent Business Owners (IBOs) would be transitioned into Amway shocked me. This was unacceptable for several reasons. For one thing, I was not in Amway (having purposefully not renewed when Quixtar launched), nor did I want to be in Amway. For another, I had told tens of thousands of people that they were Independent Business Owners affiliated with Quixtar just as the IBO moniker implied. True, Quixtar was owned by the founders of Amway, but they were allegedly separate companies with separate field organizations. Indeed, I must have repeated this message of separate companies a thousand times because that is what Ken McDonald and the rest of Quixtar's management team had told all of us. In sum, the deal had either been changed, or I had been misled and thus found myself in the inadvertent position of being asked to likewise do so to others.

For me, the whole conflict was a moral issue. On one hand, I knew Quixtar (like any company) had the power to break its commitments to its customers, but it didn't have the power to avoid the subsequent fallout. On the other hand, how could I represent a company to others that I believed had misrepresented itself to me? Indeed, leadership is character in motion, and without trust, it's impossible for any leader to get in motion. Nevertheless, quitting my independent business was not as simple as it sounded since Amway had stated its intention to litigate against any leader attempting to leave Amway/Quixtar (indeed, hundreds were sued before and after me). Not surprisingly, the legal risk intimidated many other leaders into submission, but it only emboldened our leadership team. If we stayed with Amway because we feared litigation, then we would be imprisoned into Amway's Legal Matrix and not truly independent anyway. How could we ever recommend others to join us as Independent Business Owners when we knew in our hearts that the term was no longer true?

Although the easiest thing to do would have been to rejoin Amway, announce my retirement, and slowly watch my groups dissolve, this was morally unconscionable. I also doubted Amway's antiquated business model could work in the Internet-savvy North American market regardless of how many millions Amway spent on television advertisements. (Amway no longer discloses North American sales volume, but it is rumored to have dropped precipitously.) How could Laurie and I in good conscience give up our purpose and principles for profit while our community suffered? And yet, I also knew that I would be sued by Amway (a multibillion-dollar international company) if I didn't agree to its plan. Financially, this was a lose-lose scenario. Neither option, in other words, was without massive risk and challenges, but leaders are paid to make decisions, and it was time to make a decision.

Thankfully, I had great leaders like Chris Brady, Tim Marks, Claude Hamilton, George Guzzardo, and Bill Lewis (interestingly, I barely knew my good friend and LIFE Leadership cofounder Dan Hawkins at the time), who all believed we should choose character over convenience. Accordingly, I called a meeting with Quixtar's top management to announce my immediate resignation and intention to sit out Quixtar's six-month non-compete period. My plan was to form a new company and build our businesses entirely separate from either Quixtar or Amway. Disastrously, however, instead of accepting my resignation, Amway announced it was "firing" me (how a company can fire an Independent Business Owner is still inexplicable to me) and proceeded to call each of the leaders in our community to demand they choose either Quixtar (soon to be Amway) or staying with me. Of course, the field leaders had no idea what Quixtar was talking about since I had not announced to anyone (except a handful of my top leaders) any plans to start another business.

Amway's management team had no idea the hornet's nest they had knocked over. People in our organization were already upset at the name change, and now Amway/ Quixtar compounded its errors through "firing" Chris Brady and I, manufacturing press releases, and issuing business ultimatums. Not surprisingly, Quixtar paid for its hubris. In our organization alone, over 50,000 IBOs chose to resign rather than switch to Amway. Of course, Amway (true to its promise) initiated multimillion-dollar court and arbitration proceedings against me and others. The financial stakes were high since we had already lost our business incomes and now risked bankruptcy. Evidently, the plan appeared to be to sue people into submission.

Consequently, starting our own company was out of the question. It would be foolhardy to attempt when a multibillion-dollar company was seeking to squash us. I didn't feel that falling on my own sword and hurting the many people who followed me out of Quixtar was the proper plan. Rather, I needed a plan for survival until Amway realized we would not surrender our principles no matter what the consequences. Accordingly, I sought to join another company so I could earn money to help support our growing legal mess (tens of millions of dollars). Of course, I ensured, upfront, that once the legal battles were over, we would be free to start our own business if we still desired to.

Fortunately, I found Dallin Larsen, the 2009 Ernst & Young Entrepreneur of the Year and founder of MonaVie. MonaVie, in 2008, was one of the fastest growing companies in network marketing (Dallin retired in 2014 and MonaVie was subsequently sold to Jeunesse in 2015). While he benefited from bringing in our large organization (millions of dollars per month in volume), he also had taken a huge risk. In truth, I do not see how we would have survived without working with MonaVie. As expected, Amway subsequently sued MonaVie (I commend their persistence) and countless more millions were spent battling the behemoth. Fortunately, Dallin Larsen did not flinch and followed through on everything he committed to despite several years of legal harassment.

Finally, in 2010, a global settlement was reached. After much pain and pressure (the battle had left no one unscathed) the war was over. I believe Amway finally realized the IBOs who resigned were not coming back, and we had enough funding to continue the legal battles indefinitely. As a result, the biggest leadership challenge we had ever faced was finally over. Our community was FREE! This was our team's finest moment. I have never been prouder of any group of leaders for they had survived over three years (2007 through 2010) without surrendering, some even choosing to declare bankruptcy rather than give in to Amway's legal demands.

In closing, many times during the struggle I had told the leaders that those who stayed would be champions. It is inspiring to see how many achievers stayed with us to finish the million-person mission. These men and women are the ones who dreamed, the ones who dared, and the ones who sacrificed to make LIFE Leadership a reality. Although I have read thousands of books on businesses, I have never found a more inspiring example of a group of common people willing to face uncommon giants. Perhaps the best description of the LIFE Leadership pioneers is displayed on a plaque at the Overpass Museum in Carney, Nebraska: "The cowards never started. The weak died on the way. Only the strong survived." If a person is ready to face his personal Goliaths, I know of no stronger community to help him do so than LIFE Leadership.

5. How is LIFE Leadership different from traditional network marketing companies?

This is a great question and deserves to be answered in several parts.

The majority of LIFE Leadership shares are owned by field leaders. As Chairman of the Board, I make nearly all my income from building my business asset just like you. As such, I would be crazy to do anything to harm the field leaders because I am one of them. In addition, the other founders (outside of CEO Chris Brady and President Rob Hallstrand) build the business just like everyone else and thus earn the majority of their incomes there. As a result, they will not tolerate win-lose corporate maneuvers that hurt the field leadership. The LIFE Coaches have formed a Policy Council that helps create and implement corporate policy. Since the Policy Council controls the majority of the shares of LIFE Leadership, the field is protected like no other company.

Furthermore, LIFE Leadership has structured its business where a minimum of 60% of all the revenue generated is returned to the field leaders. The remaining 40% of the revenue is broken down to 30% to run the company (office, employees, and cost of goods sold) and no more than 10% profit for the company. Importantly, the field members are ensured 60% (in 2014 the actual number was 64%) of the revenue even if the company makes no money. We created compensation structure to ensure the corporate office is fiscally conservative because its bonuses are based upon hitting the 30% figure. In a word, all boats rise together when the tide does. The reward systems were designed this way specifically because we learned firsthand what happens when corporate and field leadership have different agendas.

In essence, LIFE Leadership trademarked "Compensated Communities" in order to highlight its three main innovations compared to traditional network marketing:

INNOVATION #1: Higher compensation rates than any other system we know of, which means that everyone can have huge success. The choice is up to each member.

INNOVATION #2: We use a Team Approach to help everyone succeed in business at a whole new level. Leaders help new members market and merchandise to build the "apprenticeship team." In other words, people are in business for themselves, but not by themselves.

INNOVATION #3: Pay raises are based on performance, pure and simple. Members are paid on building communities in which products and services are merchandised. This is significant because it ensures performance rather than politics is rewarded. At LIFE Leadership, everyone knows level of performance is necessary to achieve a certain level of income. Everything is open, honest, and available to all. You get to decide if you get a raise, a promotion, and other benefits. (Please see the LIFE Leadership Compensation Plan and Income Disclosure Statement.)

INNOVATION #4: LIFE Leadership pays all incomes [compensation plan, One-Time Cash Awards (OTCAs), and Community Advancement Bonuses (CAB)] based on sales volume. There is no secret money paid to only a select group on training or support materials. To use an analogy, members are paid for completing bridges, rather than selling hammers and nails needed to build bridges. This ensures people recommend only the appropriate amount of training and support needed to accomplish a long-term sustainable business result.

I believe if the owners of network marketing companies back in the 1960s and 1970s would have disciplined themselves to only keep 10% of company income and use the other 90% to run the company and pay bonuses, network marketing would be as big as discount stores like Wal-Mart and Target today. Instead, most companies take around one-third each for profit, business operations, and field profits. In contrast, Wal-Mart is excited if they hit between 6–10% profit. The discrepancy in profits kept between discount stores and most network marketing companies is, in my opinion, the main reason network marketing has not lived up to its potential growth. Fortunately, a Compensated Community, by operating within the 60-30-10 percentages, ensures the majority of corporate revenues flow to field leaders rather than company executives. For when the company does have profits above 10%, the excess profits are paid out as bigger bonuses to field leaders the next year. As CEO Chris Brady said "We didn't found this company to make a lot of money; we founded it to pay a lot of money!"

This leads me into the final competitive advantage, namely, CEO Chris Brady. Chris is an *Inc.* magazine Top 40 leader and *New York Times* bestselling leadership author. We have been business partners and great friends for over twenty years. He is one of the most creative and character-centered people I know. After working with him for an extended period of time, I realized that he refuses to play politics, refuses to pass the buck, and has a burning desire to achieve excellence in everything he does. Indeed, I met him when we were both eighteen-year-old kids about ready to enter engineering school together, and the hunger to excel was present even back then. His friendship and business partnership has been a blessing to our family.

LIFE Leadership's corporate office is located just outside of Raleigh, North Carolina, near where Chris lives. He is responsible for leading the corporate offices, and I am responsible for leading the Compensated Community. Together, along with the rest of the Policy Council, we set the course for LIFE Leadership. Chris and I talk nearly every day to ensure the company and the field leaders are aligned in vision, culture, and objectives. I believe LIFE Leadership has the right people on the bus, in the right seats on the bus, and now we are driving onward to reach one million people with our life-changing information. We hope you're one of them!

Notes

1. *The Matrix*, released March 31, 1999 (USA), written and directed by Andy and Lana (Larry) Wachowski (as The Wachowski Brothers).

2. Ibid.

3. Ibid.

4. The material in this section came from a conversation I had with my friend and business partner Mark Haas.

5. *The Matrix*, released March 31, 1999 (USA), written and directed by Andy and Lana (Larry) Wachowski (as The Wachowski Brothers).